Bac Pro 2de

A2-B1

NEW TIP TOP ENGLISH

F. Bascou | B. Léonori | S. Ritter | B. Sirjean | S. Vitel

FOUCHER

Sommaire

UNIT 1 page 7

Meet-ups

TÂCHE FINALE Écrire des cartes postales pour un projet Postcrossing EE – A2

Structures	be / have / parler de ses goûts / le présent simple
Lexique	*a postcard, an email address, a sender... / be fond of, hate, enjoy, sign up... / favourite, scenic...*
Phonologie	la prononciation du « s » de la 3e personne du présent simple

UNIT 2 page 17

English Made Easy

TÂCHE FINALE Réaliser un tutoriel EE – A2+

Structures	*Would you like ...? / I'd like ... / Could you + V ...? /* l'impératif
Lexique	*emergency, floor, lift, lost property office... / be hungry or thirsty, need, turn right, walk past... / Can I help you? Let me know if...*
Phonologie	la prononciation des mots à consonne muette

ISBN 978-2-216-14844-8

CitySightseeing London

Sommaire

UNIT 5 – Fabulous India
page 55

TÂCHE FINALE Réaliser un jeu de *Jeopardy* EE – A2+

Structures le prétérit / le comparatif de supériorité

Lexique *currency, flag, issue, trade… / become, begin, date back to, lead, take control of… / lively, noisy / formerly, yet / dozens of, thousands of, twice…*

Phonologie la prononciation des mots interrogatifs

UNIT 6 – Smart Cities
page 65

TÂCHE FINALE Présenter une ville intelligente à l'aide d'un diaporama EOC – A2+

Structures le superlatif, l'obligation, la possibilité ou l'impossibilité

Lexique *an app, waste, a recycling bin… / check, upgrade, recycle… / smart, polluting*

Phonologie la prononciation de *can, can't, must, mustn't*

UNIT 7 page 79

From Startups to Giants

TÂCHE FINALE Présenter une startup à partir d'une *mind map* EOC – A2+

Structures les adverbes *already, never, not... yet* / le *present perfect*

Lexique *a career, a CEO, a device... / design, found, provide... / smart, innovative... / already, never...*

Phonologie la prononciation des sons /ɒ/, /aʊ/, /ʌ/

UNIT 8 page 89

Native Americans

TÂCHE FINALE Présenter une tribu amérindienne EOC – B1

Structures le présent en *-ing* / *could* / *had to*

Lexique *an arrow, a reservation, a warrior... / fight, appease, defeat... / peaceful... / in the background...*

Phonologie la prononciation des lettres « ea »

Sommaire

UNIT 9 – page 103
The Roaring Twenties

TÂCHE FINALE Présenter un aspect des années 1920 EOC - B1

Structures les pronoms relatifs, *used to*

Lexique *smuggling, a bootlegger / drink, fail, ban…*

Phonologie la prononciation de la lettre « h »

UNIT 10 – page 113
Thrilling Stories

TÂCHE FINALE Écrire un récit à suspense EE - B1

Structures les connecteurs, le prétérit en *-ing*

Lexique *a burglary, a fight, a murder… / investigate, patrol, shout… / safe…*

Phonologie la prononciation de la lettre « a »

UNIT 1

TÂCHE FINALE Écrire des cartes postales pour un projet Postcrossing

EE – A2

Meet-ups

© hopscotchtheglobe.com

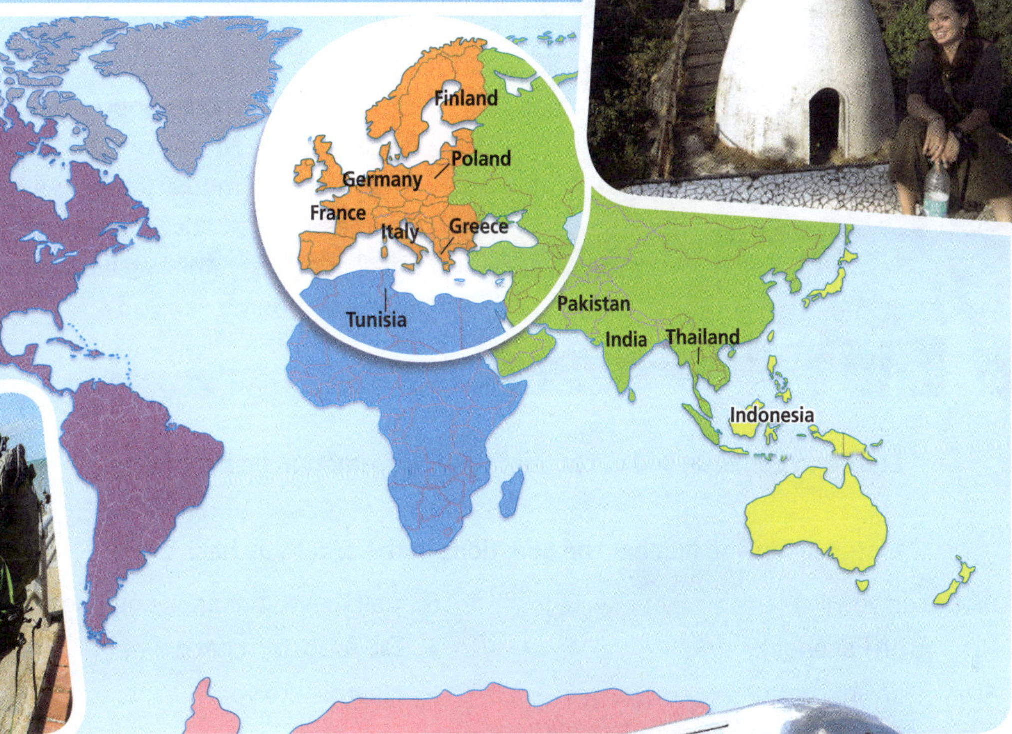

© hopscotchtheglobe.com

Colour	Continent	Colour	Continent
(blue)	....	(green)	....
(pink)	....	(purple)	....
(orange)	....	(yellow)	....

1 1 Track 1 **Listen and tick the correct answers.**

a. The document is about:
☐ Kristen and Siya ☐ Christie and Maya

b. They are: ☐ Australian ☐ Canadian

c. They live in: ☐ an Airstream ☐ a mobile home

d. They are: ☐ travel vloggers ☐ travel agents

2 1 Track 1 **Listen again and circle on the map the places the vloggers visited.**

3 **Write the names of the continents in the legend.**
Africa – Europe – Asia – America – Oceania – Antarctica

BREAK IN VIDEO

vidéo
Welcome to the Travel Vlogger – 1'40''
foucherconnect.fr/18tten01

a. **Travelling is:**
☐ only a passion for the travel vlogger
☐ a passion and his job

b. **He has already travelled to:**
☐ 30 ☐ 40 countries.

c. **He works:**
☐ alone ☐ with sponsors and big companies

Follow Me!

Activity A Cameron's Presentation

Cameron Patterson
Sex: male / female
Age: 15 / 16 / 17
Occupation: student / apprentice
Place of living: Miami, USA / Stratford, UK
Favorite social media: Instagram / Facebook
Hobbies: playing video games / chatting online
Email address: cuteboy@lifewire.net / goodboy@mail.com
Phone number: 974 6963 / 987 6543

1 1 Track 2 **Listen to Cameron and circle the correct information on his profile.**

2 1 Track 2 **Listen again and number the questions in the order you hear them.**

a. Where do you live? ....
b. Are you on Facebook? ....
c. Are you an apprentice? ....
d. Can I have your phone number? ....
e. Do you often chat online? ....
f. How old are you? ....

Activity B Express Yourself with Emojis

a. b. c. d. e. f.

3 **Match the emojis and their meaning.**

1. I'm fond of clothes, shoes and pets. → ....
2. I enjoy music, sport and partying. → ....
3. I love my family, boxing and coffee! → ....
4. I'm in love with Jack. → ....
5. My birthday is on the fifteenth of March. → ....
6. I hate going to the swimming pool. → ....

4 1 Track 3 **Listen and write the messages using emojis.**

a.	b.	c.

Activity C **Profile Bios**

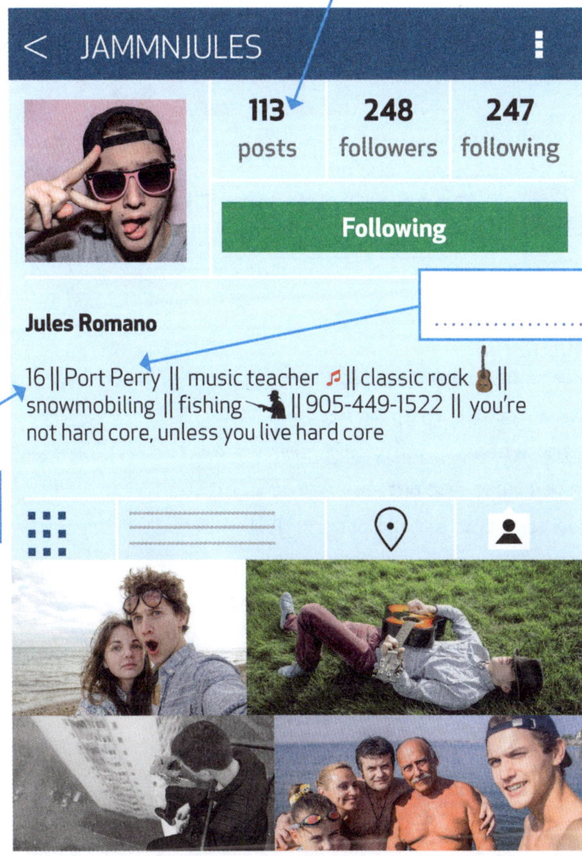

5 **Fill in the labels with:** *number of followers – user name – number of published documents – place of living – school level – age*

6 **Read the profile bios and answer the questions.**

a. Who is in a relationship?

....

b. Is music only a hobby for Jules?

....

c. Who is more popular on Instagram?

....

....

7 **Complete the description of Grace's profile.**

Her .... is Grace-Neill. She is in grade .... at school, so she is about 15 years old.
She is .... with a boy named Tom.
She is a fan of the .... boys band BTS. She .... her friends and her family. Her favourite .... are cheerleading and softball.
She .... the motto* *Hakuna Matata* from the movie *The Lion King*. It means ...., that is to say: make the most of every moment.

* *devise*

8 **Present Jules's profile orally.**

FOCUS

a. **I am seventeen.**

- *Pour indiquer son âge, on utilise :*

☐ *have* ☐ *be*

b. **He doesn't like playing baseball. I enjoy partying.**

- *Soulignez les verbes conjugués.*
- *De quoi sont-ils suivis?* ....

Training ex. 1, 3, 5

NOW ACT

9 **Write and present your Instagram profile bio.**
Give indication about your place of living (not your full address!), age, birthday, occupation, hobbies, pets, motto… You can do it on your mobile phone and do a screen capture or go to **page 134**. Then present it to your partner orally.

Postcrossing

Activity D Postcard from Florida

....

Hi Justin,
My name is Deborah, I'm 18, I'm in 12th grade* and I study graphic design. My hobbies are drawing, painting, sewing and travelling. I have one cat, his name is Jupiter.
I hope you like this scenic postcard; it shows the beach next to my home. I spend lots of summer evenings there with my friends playing beach volleyball. This month I did a three-week placement with an advertising company, which was great. When I leave school, I hope to become a publicist.
I wish you all the best,

Deborah XXX

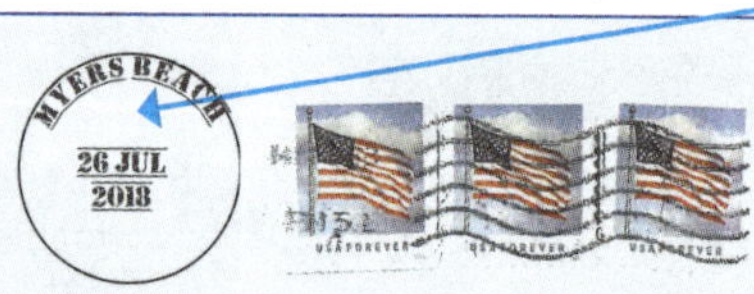

....

....

....

Justin Robert
17, place de la liberté
55100 VERDUN
FRANCE

....

Fort Myers Beach, Florida. *Located on Estero Island is Fort Myers Beach and Pier. This beach has the reputation of being one of the safest due to its warm shallow waters and no undertow. The pier is a popular destination for fishing, watching the dolphins play or enjoying the spectacular sunsets. Photo by Martin Gordash*

....

* *last year of high school*

1 Select the correct answers.

a. The document is:
☐ a postcard ☐ a letter from Florida

b. Justin and Deborah:
☐ are long-standing friends
☐ don't know each other

2 Fill in the labels with:
addressee's postal address – name of the sender – stamps – date – information about the place shown on the card – greetings

3 Find the English equivalents in the document.

a. *le graphisme* : ....
b. *la couture* : ....
c. *un stage* : ....
d. *une entreprise de publicité* : ....
....

NOW ACT

5 Read the postcard page 127 and say in French what you have understood.

4 True or false? Underline the information in the document.

	True	False
a. Deborah likes astrology.	☐	☐
b. She didn't enjoy her work placement in an advertising company.	☐	☐
c. Her professional project is to work in publicity.	☐	☐

FOCUS

a. I study graphic design.
b. It shows the beach next to my home.

- *Soulignez les verbes conjugués.*
- *À quel temps sont-ils ?* ....
- *À quelle personne faut-il ajouter un '-s' au verbe ?*

....

Training ex. 4

TÂCHE 3 Comprendre le témoignage d'une abonnée à un site

CO – B1

VIDEO TIME 1

World Greetings

vidéo
Postcrossing – 3'24''
foucherconnect.fr/18tten02

Step 1 Before watching the video.

1 Read the title of the video, look at the picture above and answer the questions.

a. What does the picture show?

....

b. What do you think the video will be about?

....

....

Step 2 Watch the whole video.

2 Answer the questions.

a. What is Hannah talking about?

....

....

b. How many postcards are pinned on the map of the world?

....

c. How many postcards does Hannah show?

....

HELP!

get* involved s'engager
an owl un hibou
postage l'affranchissement
a random person une personne aléatoire
scenic pittoresque
sign up s'inscrire, s'abonner
weird bizarre, étrange

Step 3 Watch the video up to 0:30.

3 Complete the script.

a. One of my .... hobbies is collecting .... from all around the ....

b. I got involved with this .... through a .... called Postcrossing.

c. The aim of the .... is you send a postcard and you .... a postcard from a random .... in the world.

Step 4 Watch the video from 0:31 to 0:47.

4 Say if these statements are true or false.

	True	False
a. Hannah likes Postcrossing because she can choose the country where the postcard is going to come from.	☐	☐
b. She finds some postcards are weird and others lovely.	☐	☐
c. She shows her postcards in the hope people will sign up.	☐	☐

Fiche VIDEO TIME 1 *Postcrossing* complète disponible en téléchargement

UNIT 1

Training

#exo foucherconnect.fr/18tten03

IN TUNE

A Track 4 **Écoutez les différentes prononciations du « s » de la 3e personne du présent simple.**

/z/ loves - /s/ likes - /iz/ dances

B Track 5 **Écoutez et complétez avec /z/, /s/ ou /iz/.**

a. he enjoys /...../ **b.** she paints /...../ **c.** he travels /...../

d. she chats /...../ **e.** he brushes /...../ **f.** he works /...../

1 **Complétez avec *be* ou *have* conjugués au présent.**

a. Her name .... Zhuldiz. She .... 27.

b. She .... from Mongolia.

c. She .... two children named Hulan and Kayla.

d. She .... long black hair and brown eyes.

e. She .... fond of watching horror films.

2 **En vous aidant des drapeaux, écrivez le nom des pays, puis remettez les lettres orangées dans l'ordre pour trouver le pays mystère.**

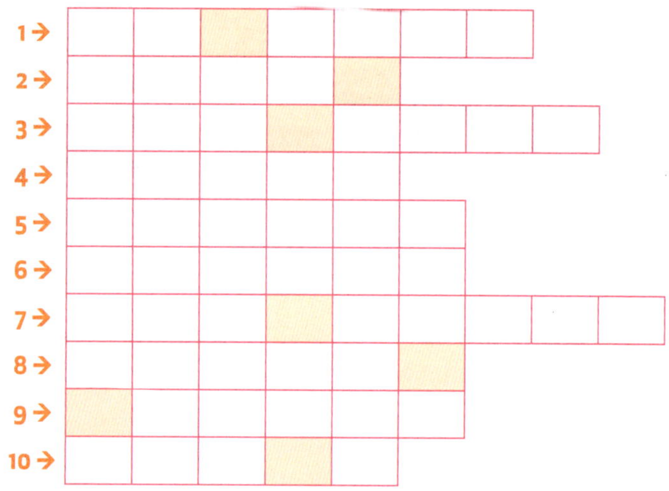

1

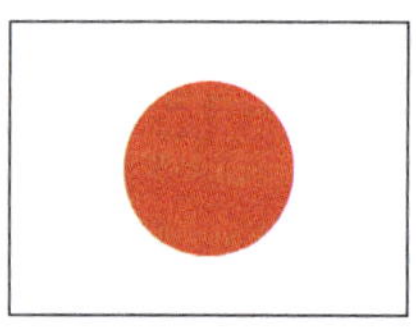
2

3

4

5

6

7

8

9

10

Pays mystère : ....

Vocabulary

Nouns

an addressee un destinataire
a country un pays
an email address une adresse électronique
a follower un abonné
an occupation une profession, un métier
a password un mot de passe
a postcard une carte postale
a sender un expéditeur
social media les réseaux sociaux
a stamp un timbre
a user ID un identifiant
a website un site internet

Verbs

be* fond of aimer
chat tchatter, bavarder
enjoy aimer, apprécier
hate détester
live habiter
party faire la fête
sign up s'inscrire, s'abonner
travel voyager

Adjectives

favourite préféré
popular populaire
single célibataire

Others

at (@) arobase
dot (.) point (mail, site)

3 1 Track 6 **Complétez les énoncés avec les mots suivants :** *playing – going out – chatting – post – love.* **Écoutez et vérifiez.**

a. I like .... on Facebook.

b. I .... messages on Instagram every day.

c. I .... looking at photos on Snapchat.

d. Her hobbies are riding her horse and .... with her friends.

e. I don't like .... video games.

4 Conjuguez les verbes au présent simple.

a. Kevin .... with his parents and his sister in a small Irish village. *(live)*

b. Tina's parents .... her passion for motorbikes. *(not like)*

c. She .... to become a sales assistant after her exam. *(hope)*

d. Sarah .... to go to the swimming pool because she .... swimming. *(not want / hate)*

e. As soon as he .... a Postcrossing postcard, he will send another one. *(receive)*

5 Rédigez au moins deux énoncés par image pour parler de vos goûts.

a

b

a. ....

....

....

....

....

....

....

b. ....

....

....

....

....

....

....

Language TIPS

Be (être) au présent

→ Forme affirmative

I am / I'm	**It is** / It's
You are / You're	**We are** / We're
He is / He's	**They are** / They're
She is / She's	

→ Forme négative

I'm not... *je ne suis pas...*

→ Forme interrogative

Are you... ?
Est-ce que tu es / vous êtes... ?

Have (avoir) au présent

→ Forme affirmative

I have / you have / he, she, it has / we have / you have / they have

→ Forme négative

I don't have... *Je n'ai pas...*

→ Forme interrogative

Do you have... ? *Est-ce que tu as / vous avez... ?*

Le présent simple

→ Forme affirmative

I study business. *J'étudie le commerce.*

He wants to travel. *Il veut voyager.*

→ Forme négative

I don't have a Facebook account.
Je n'ai pas de compte Facebook.

She doesn't have Snapchat.
Elle n'a pas Snapchat.

Parler de ses goûts

I like social networks.
J'aime les réseaux sociaux.

She enjoys / She's fond of partying.
Elle aime faire la fête.

I don't like / I hate playing handball.
Je n'aime pas / Je déteste jouer au handball.

I hate broccoli. *Je déteste les brocolis.*

FINAL TASK 1 Take Part in a Postcrossing Project

SCENARIO Dans le cadre de l'ouverture internationale de votre établissement, vous devez vous inscrire sur le site Postcrossing afin d'envoyer et de recevoir des cartes postales du monde entier.

Étape 1 Remplir un formulaire pour créer son profil EE - A1+

- Inscrivez-vous sur le site www.postcrossing.com pour créer votre fiche profil. Validez votre inscription afin de recevoir les coordonnées de la personne à qui vous allez envoyer votre première carte postale.

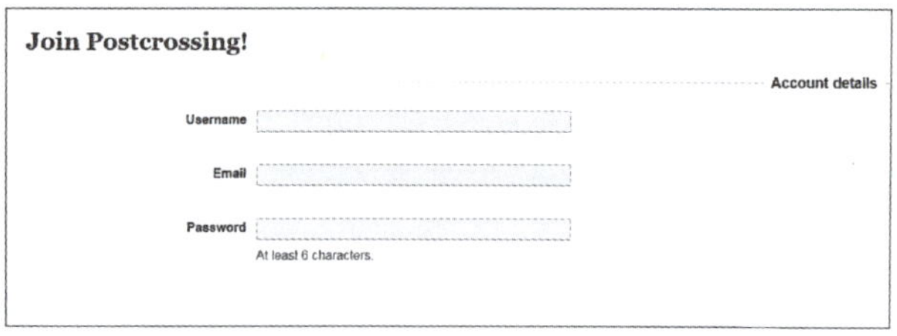
Join Postcrossing!

Account details

Username

Email

Password

At least 6 characters.

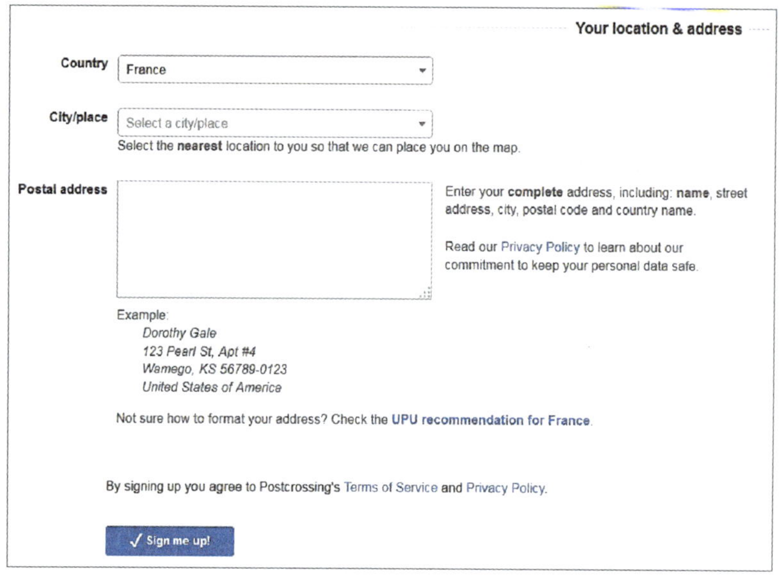
Your location & address

Country: France

City/place: Select a city/place
Select the **nearest** location to you so that we can place you on the map.

Postal address

Enter your **complete** address, including: **name**, street address, city, postal code and country name.

Read our Privacy Policy to learn about our commitment to keep your personal data safe.

Example:
Dorothy Gale
123 Pearl St, Apt #4
Wamego, KS 56789-0123
United States of America

Not sure how to format your address? Check the **UPU recommendation for France**.

By signing up you agree to Postcrossing's Terms of Service and Privacy Policy.

✓ Sign me up!

Étape 2 Écrire une carte postale EE - A2+

- Notez l'adresse de la personne à qui vous allez envoyer votre carte postale et le code ID fourni par le site (code nécessaire pour comptabiliser le nombre de cartes reçues et envoyées).

....

- Consultez le profil de cette personne.
- Préparez le brouillon de votre carte postale. Vous pouvez parler de vous, de vos loisirs, de vos études…
- Après avoir relu votre message, recopiez-le ainsi que l'adresse sur votre carte postale, en prenant soin d'écrire lisiblement. Postez votre carte postale (n'oubliez pas le timbre !).
- Attendez de recevoir à votre tour une carte postale et vous pourrez l'afficher (autour d'un planisphère, par exemple).

mon bilan UNIT 1

	J'ai réussi à…	−−	−	+	++
EOC	Me présenter à partir d'un profil				
CE	Comprendre le contenu d'une carte postale				
CO	Comprendre le témoignage d'un(e) abonné(e) à un site				
EE	Remplir un formulaire				
EE	Écrire une carte postale				

UNIT 1 S'exprimer à partir d'un formulaire

LET'S TRAIN!

1 Track 7 **Lisez le document. Puis écoutez la présentation orale qui en est faite et complétez.**

His .... John Smith. He .... in the United States, in New York City. His .... is 6 Manhattan Square. The .... is 10044. His .... is smitj and his .... is 2sunshine. His .... is john.smith@nyu.com. He is .... in the www.gamespot.com .... because he .... playing video games. His .... console is Xbox One. He is a football player and he .... the Fifa 18 game. He is also .... adventure games like Destiny 2.

Sign up — www.gamespot.com

User ID	smitj
Password	2sunshine
Name	SMITH John
Address	6 Manhattan Square NEW YORK CITY
Country	US
ZIP code	10044
Email	john.smith@nyu.com
Sex	☒ Male ☐ Femelle
Language	☒ English ☐ Non English
About	Love playing video games. Favorite console: Xbox One Best games: Fifa 18 (because I'm a football player) and adventure games like Destiny 2.

Submit

2 **Entraînez-vous à lire et à répéter la présentation ci-dessus.**

3 **Présentez John Smith sans modèle.**

YOUR TURN!

SIGN-UP FORM — www.techstyle.com

ACCOUNT DETAILS		PROFILE DETAILS	
Username:	doro16	Gender:	female
Email:	dorothy.pirkins@bt.com	Marital status:	single
Password:	178dpS	Hobbies / Leisure:	fashion, online chats, handball

IDENTITY		YOUR LOCATION AND ADDRESS	
Name:	Dorothy Pirkins	Country:	England
Age:	16	City/Place:	Winchester
Occupation:	student		

4 **Utilisez les informations du profil pour présenter oralement cette personne. Entraînez-vous, enregistrez-vous et réécoutez votre présentation pour essayer de l'améliorer.**

CCF PREP 2

PARTIE 2 EOI

S'entraîner à répondre à des questions sur une personne

LET'S TRAIN!

A very sporty boy!

♥ chatting on the Net

He is a fan of punk rock.

1 Track 8 Observez les documents pour répondre aux questions enregistrées.

a. ....

b. ....

c. ....

d. ....

e. ....

Name: Terence Barry
Place of living: Nottingham, UK
Age: 18
Status: in a relationship with Kelly
Occupation: student in musicology

YOUR TURN!

2 Observez les documents. Posez trois questions sur Taylor à votre partenaire, puis répondez à votre tour à ses questions.

Name: Taylor Swap
Age: 15
Home: Houston, US
Sports practised: skateboarding and dancing
Status: not in a relationship at the moment

UNIT
2

TÂCHE FINALE → **Réaliser un tutoriel**

EE – A2+

English Made Easy

TRAVEL ESSENTIALS

☐ ....

☐ ID card

☐ plane tickets

☐ bookings

☐ ....

☐ ....

☐ travel insurance

☐ emergency numbers

TECHNOLOGY CHECKLIST

☐ ....

☐ phone charger

☐ ....

☐ tablet

☐ camera

☐ ....

1 **Complete the document with the following elements.**
passport – smartphone – credit card – plug adapter – cash – earphones

2 **Match the words and their translations.**

a. ID card ○ ○ **1.** réservations
b. bookings ○ ○ **2.** numéros d'urgence
c. travel insurance ○ ○ **3.** carte d'identité
d. emergency numbers ○ ○ **4.** assurance voyage

3 1 Track 9 **Listen and tick on the list what James takes.**

BREAK IN VIDEO

 # vidéo
How to Pack a Suitcase to Maximize Space – 1'18''
foucherconnect.fr/18tten04

a. The video is about how to pack:
☐ a large suitcase
☐ a backpack

b. Lacy recommends:
☐ rolling clothes ☐ folding clothes

c. The heaviest items should be put:
☐ at the top ☐ in the middle
☐ at the bottom

UNIT 2

TÂCHE 1 **Établir un contact social pour demander ou fournir une aide**

EOI – A2+

Making Your Own Way

Activity A First Meeting

1 1 Track 10 **Listen and write down what Fred and his host say.**

a. ....

b. Would you like ....? Would you like .... or ....?

c. I'd like ...., please.

d. Here is a .... for you. I .... you will like it.

e. That's very ....

Activity B Giving Directions

2 1 Track 11 **Listen and complete the sentences.**

a. Excuse me… Could you tell me the .... to the supermarket, please?

b. Go straight .... Walk .... the bank. The supermarket is .... the fast food restaurant.

c. Go .... The shoe store is .... the coffee bar.

d. Please, could you .... me directions to the cinema?

e. Take the .... The cinema is on the .... floor. Turn right. It's ....

3 1 Track 11 **Listen again. Trace the three ways and locate the places on the map.**

Activity C What To Say If...

4 1 Track 12 **Match the sentences and the situations on the right (1 – 2 – 3). Then listen and check.**

a. There has been a car accident. We need help!: → ....
b. Sorry, I don't think I have got the time: → ....
c. Excuse me. I wonder if you could help me. Has anyone found my key?: → ....
d. Thank you. But I'm afraid I can't: → ....
e. Please let me know if anyone finds it: → ....
f. Could you come as soon as possible?: → ....

1. You want to refuse politely

2. You have lost something

3. There is an emergency

Activity D At the Lost Property Office

5 1 Track 13 **Listen and complete the dialogues. Then write the corresponding picture numbers.**

a.
- .... me. I wonder if you could help me. Has anyone ....?
- A phone? ...., I have no phone here. .... did you lose it? → Picture n°.........

b.
- Please, could you help me? I've ....!
- Oh! I'm .... You can go to the lost property office. → Picture n°........

c.
- I .... Not a long time .... I think.
- .... me your contact details and I'll .... in case we find it. → Picture n°.....

d.
- Could you ...., please?
- Go .... The lost property office is .... the bank. → Picture n°.........

6 **Act the dialogue.**

FOCUS

a. Would you like a drink? Yes, I'd like a cup of tea.
b. Could you tell me the way to the supermarket?

- *Comment dire :*

- *« Pourriez-vous… ? »* ....
- *« Aimeriez/voudriez-vous… ? »* ....
- *« Je voudrais »* ....

c. Turn left. **d. Don't forget your passport.**

- *Les deux verbes sont à :*

☐ *l'infinitif* ☐ *l'impératif*

Ils expriment :

☐ *une consigne, un ordre* ☐ *une possibilité*

Training ex. 1, 3, 4

NOW ACT

7 **Work in pairs. Use the information and the pictures on page 128 to act dialogues.**

How to Order a Meal

Activity E At the Taco Shop!

1 **Tick the correct information.**

a. This document is:
☐ a cartoon ☐ a comic strip

b. Bella and Jamie are having:
☐ a drink ☐ a meal together at the taco shop.

2 **Use the vocabulary in the comic strip to fill in the labels.**

 ....  ....  ....

 ....  ....

3 **Find in the document the English for:**

a. *Que puis-je faire pour vous ?* ....
b. *très épicé* ....
c. *à emporter* ....
d. *Je prendrai* ....
e. *Voici pour vous* ....
f. *Bon appétit !* ....
g. *Miam !* ....

4 **Tick "True" or "False".**

	True	False
a. Jamie is ordering a hot taco.	☐	☐
b. Bella will have a fish soft taco.	☐	☐
c. They want to eat in.	☐	☐
d. Jamie will have soda.	☐	☐
e. They are not sure the tacos are good.	☐	☐

NOW ACT

5 **Write a dialogue to fill in the comic strip on page 128.**

VIDEO TIME 2

At the Clothes Shop

 # vidéo
Conversation Tips: Shopping for Clothes – 1'24''
foucherconnect.fr/18tten05

Step 1 Before watching the video.

1 Look at the picture above and read the title of the video. Then make hypotheses about the topic of the video.

....

....

....

....

HELP!

a clerk (US) un vendeur, une vendeuse
drama théâtre/art dramatique
gorgeous superbe, splendide
high-end haut de gamme
an item un article (commerce)
leather le cuir
props des accessoires
scenery un décor (théâtre)
a shopper un(e) client(e)

Step 2 Watch the whole video.

2 Tick the corresponding information.

a. In the first part of the video, the man who is speaking is:
☐ an English teacher
☐ a drama coach

b. In the second part of the video, the two actors are:
☐ in a real clothing store
☐ in a scenery clothing store

Step 3 Watch the video up to 0:19.

3 Answer the questions.

a. What is the name of the drama coach?

....

b. Where are the actors in this scene?

....

c. What are the two roles the actors will play?

....

....

4 Tick "True" or "False".

	True	False
a. A high-end clothing store is a very expensive store.	☐	☐
b. The drama coach only speaks to the two actors.	☐	☐
c. The drama coach wants to explain the audience how to act in this scene.	☐	☐

Fiche VIDEO TIME 2 *At the Clothes Shop* complète disponible en téléchargement

Training

exo
foucherconnect.fr/18tten06

IN TUNE

A Track 14 **Écoutez la prononciation des mots ci-dessous et soulignez les consonnes qui ne sont pas prononcées. Puis répétez.**

could – walk – would – know – talk – listen

B Track 15 **Entraînez-vous à prononcer les énoncés suivants. Puis écoutez et vérifiez.**

a. Would you like to stop talking and listen to me, please?
b. Could you let me know if you find it?
c. Walk past the store, and then go straight on.

1 Track 16 **Complétez les légendes de ces illustrations. Puis écoutez et vérifiez.**

a. Go .... on

b. Turn ....

c. It's ....

d. Walk .... the…

e. Go ....

f. Go ....

g. Take the ....

h. It's on the ....

2 **Rayez les sept mots illustrés dans la grille de mots cachés. Puis écrivez la phrase mystère à l'aide des lettres restantes.**

D	P	L	E	A	S	E	D
O	N	T	F	O	R	S	G
K	C	A	P	K	C	A	B
N	E	K	C	I	H	C	E
T	Y	O	U	R	B	T	G
O	O	K	I	T	F	I	L
N	G	T	I	C	F	U	K
E	P	A	S	T	T	S	S

Phrase mystère : ....

Vocabulary

Nouns

a backpack un sac à dos
contact details les coordonnées
an emergency une urgence
a floor un étage
a lift un ascenseur
lost property office bureau des objets trouvés
a meal un repas
a prop un accessoire (théâtre)
a suitcase une valise

Verbs

be* hungry/thirsty avoir faim/soif
be* cold/hot avoir froid/chaud
find* trouver
forget* oublier
go* straight on aller tout droit
go* upstairs/downstairs monter/descendre (escalier)
lose* perdre
need avoir besoin de
pack faire ses bagages
turn right/left tourner à droite/gauche
walk past passer devant

Adjectives

kind gentil
pleased ravi, content
tired fatigué

Others

as soon as possible dès que possible
Can I help you? Que puis-je faire pour vous ?
in case… au cas où…
It's on your right/left C'est à votre droite/gauche
Let me know if… Faites-moi savoir si…
Nice to meet you Enchanté
I'll have (a drink) Je prendrai (une boisson)

3 **Écrivez les consignes en mettant les verbes à l'impératif et à la forme négative.**

a. (turn)

....

b. (go)

....

c. (use)

....

4 **Écrivez les questions correspondant aux réponses données.**

a. – ....

....

- Certainly. Walk past the bank. The shopping centre is on your right.

b. – ....

....

- Yes, please. I'll have a cheese sandwich.

5 **Écrivez ce que vous diriez dans les cas suivants.**

a. Vous rencontrez quelqu'un pour la première fois.

....

b. Vous voulez proposer votre aide.

....

c. Vous préférez refuser de jouer au tennis car vous n'aimez pas trop.

....

d. Vous venez de recevoir un cadeau.

....

e. Vous demandez à quelqu'un de venir le plus vite possible. Vous avez besoin d'aide.

....

....

6 **Choisissez dans le menu ce que vous voudriez commander et répondez au serveur.**

a. *Waiter*: Would you like a salad?

You: Yes, please. I ....

....

b. *Waiter*: Would you like a classic burger?

You: No, thank you. I ....

....

c. *Waiter*: Would you like a drink?

You: Yes, please, I ....

....

Language TIPS

Would you like...?

→ **proposer à manger, à boire**

What would you like? Would you like a drink? *Que voudriez-vous / voudrais-tu ? Voudriez-vous / Voudrais-tu une boisson ?*

I'd like...

→ **indiquer ce que l'on voudrait, aimerait**

I'd like a cup of coffee, please. I'd like some rest. *Je voudrais un café, s'il vous plait. J'aimerais me reposer.*

Could you + V...?

→ **demander un service**

Could you help me? Could you tell me the way to the bus stop, please?

Pourriez-vous / Pourrais-tu m'aider? Pourriez-vous m'indiquer comment aller à l'arrêt de bus, s'il vous plait ?

L'impératif

→ **donner une consigne, un ordre**

Walk past the park.
Go straight on.
Don't turn right.

Passez / Passe devant le parc.
Continuez / Continue tout droit.
Ne tournez / tourne pas à droite.

FINAL TASK 2 Create a Tuto

SCENARIO Pour préparer un futur séjour dans un pays anglophone ou l'accueil d'élèves étrangers, vous devez créer un tutoriel pour communiquer dans des situations diverses de la vie quotidienne.

Étape 1 Compléter une fiche pour réaliser un tutoriel EE – A2+

▸ Par groupe, choisissez une situation que votre tutoriel va mettre en scène (acheter dans un magasin / acheter un titre de transport / demander de l'aide / indiquer un itinéraire…) et complétez la fiche.

Tutorial: How to	
Setting:	Place: .... Time: ....
Characters: roles and names	**1.** .... **2.** .... **3.** .... **4.** ....
Initial situation **Final situation**	....
List of props (objects to help you act)	....

Étape 2 Rédiger le script d'un tutoriel EE – A2+

▸ Distribuez les rôles. Préparez des répliques courtes pour chacun. Votre tutoriel doit durer au minimum 1 minute.

▸ Utilisez les expressions et le vocabulaire qui vous paraissent indispensables dans cette situation. Utilisez un dictionnaire si besoin. Relisez attentivement.

Étape 3 Réaliser un tutoriel EOC – A2+

▸ Mémorisez vos répliques. Entraînez-vous à jouer votre saynète.

▸ Soignez la scénarisation (accessoires, tenue, voix, gestes…). Puis filmez-vous quand vous serez prêts.

▸ Déposez votre vidéo sur le site ou l'ENT du lycée.

mon bilan UNIT 2

	J'ai réussi à…	▫▫	▫	+	++
EOI	Établir un contact social pour demander ou fournir une aide				
EE	Rédiger un dialogue de BD				
CO	Comprendre des conseils pour jouer un sketch				
EOI	Réaliser un tutoriel				

UNIT 2

Théâtraliser un énoncé

CCF PREP 3

PARTIE 1 EOC

LET'S TRAIN!

1 Track 17 Écoutez attentivement la même phrase dite quatre fois de façon différente et notez l'effet apporté (compréhensible ou incompréhensible ? audible ou inaudible ? suscite l'intérêt ou le rejet ?).

a. ....

b. ....

c. ....

d. ....

Living abroad will help build foreign connections and develop your understanding of varying cultural needs – two crucial skills in the professional world.

2 Track 18 Écoutez une autre phrase prononcée trois fois et exprimant à chaque fois un sentiment différent. Notez la lettre (A, B, ou C) correspondant au sentiment exprimé.

Conviction, sérieux : ......

Tristesse : ......

Enthousiasme, joie : ......

3 Track 17 Track 18 Réécoutez les deux énoncés. Entraînez-vous à les répéter de différentes façons, en exprimant différents sentiments.

YOUR TURN!

"A journey of a thousand miles must begin with a single step."

4 Préparez-vous à dire l'énoncé ci-dessus. Parlez de façon audible et compréhensible. Choisissez le sentiment que vous souhaitez exprimer. Puis enregistrez-vous.

5 Par deux, rédigez d'autres énoncés et entraînez-vous à les dire avec conviction et sérieux, ou avec enthousiasme et joie. Puis enregistrez-vous.

CCF PREP 4

PARTIE 3 CE

Comprendre un article sur une méthode d'apprentissage

LET'S TRAIN!

How to Learn a New Language Fast

1. Connect with a native speaker. The best way to learn a new language is to speak it. Too often, people spend their time studying grammar and memorizing lists of words instead of[1] [...] putting what they've learned into practice.

2. Study the language every day. That is, in the space of a few weeks or months — you're going to have to commit[2] to studying the language for a couple of hours per day.

3. Carry a dictionary at all times. It can be an actual, physical dictionary, or a dictionary app on your phone — you just need to be able to consult it quickly whenever you need a word.

4. Watch, listen, read and write in your chosen language. Immersing yourself in a language means doing all of the activities you would normally do in your native tongue, through your new language — whether that's reading, writing or listening.

5. Visit a country where your chosen language is spoken. It would be a great boost to your language learning skills if you could visit and spend some time in a country where your new language is spoken.

www.wikihow.com.

1. au lieu de ; 2. s'engager à

1. Quel est le sujet du document ?

....

2. Faut-il uniquement étudier la grammaire ou y a-t-il un meilleur moyen de progresser ?

....

....

3. Combien de temps va durer cet apprentissage ?

....

....

4. Comment est-il possible de s'immerger dans une langue étrangère sans quitter son pays ?

....

....

5. Quels sont les autres conseils donnés ?

....

....

American High School Traditions

Culture CLICK 1

HOMECOMING

At the .... of the school year, high school students and .... graduates[1] gather to .... their high schools. It's a .... celebration which occurs in September or October and ends with a big .... called Homecoming Dance.
Homecoming usually .... around a football game which .... with a cheerleader show to .... the school team and a performance by the school marching band.

1 Track 19 **Listen and complete the document.**

2 **Use the vocabulary in the document to write a caption under each picture.**

1. *diplômés*

GRADUATION DAY

At the end of 12th grade[1], graduates wear a cap and gown in the school's official colors. They march up onto a stage to receive their diplomas from the headmaster[2]. After the giving of diplomas, there is the "tassel turning": students move their cap tassel[3] from the right to the left, which symbolizes that they are officially graduated. At the end of the ceremony, all graduates throw their caps into the air to celebrate their new status.

1. *terminale (US)* ; 2. *proviseur(e)* ; 3. *pompon*

3 **Read the document and answer the questions.**

a. When does Graduation Day occur? ....
b. What do students usually wear? ....
c. Who gives out the diplomas? ....
d. What do students do at the end of the ceremony? ....

4 **Write the corresponding letter (a or b).**

Place of the tassel: *before* (......) *after* (......) graduation

Quiz

1 American teens usually start High School at the age of:
- **a.** 12 ☐
- **b.** 13 ☐
- **c.** 14 ☐

2 A first-year high school student is called:
- **a.** a freshman ☐
- **b.** an alumnus ☐
- **c.** a senior ☐

3 A final-year high school student is called:
- **a.** a sophomore ☐
- **b.** a junior ☐
- **c.** a senior ☐

4 "Winter Formal" is:
- **a.** a sports event ☐
- **b.** a parade ☐
- **c.** a dance ☐

5 "Prom" is short for:
- **a.** Promposal ☐
- **b.** Promenade ☐
- **c.** Promise ☐

6 Prom was born in:
- **a.** the early 1800s ☐
- **b.** the early 1900s ☐
- **c.** the late 1900s ☐

7 She had her prom at the White House (1975):
- **a.** President Obama's daughter ☐
- **b.** President Ford's daughter ☐
- **c.** President Clinton's daughter ☐

8 A "mortar board' is:
- **a.** an academic gown ☐
- **b.** an academic cap ☐
- **c.** a stole *(une étole)* ☐

9 "Pomp and Circumstance" is:
- **a.** a novel ☐
- **b.** a ceremony ☐
- **c.** the graduation theme song ☐

10 The average amount spent by a teen on a prom is:
- **a.** less than $250 ☐
- **b.** $500 ☐
- **c.** $1500 ☐

1 Track 21 **Listen and check.**

Your score: … /10

PROM TIME

5 1 Track 20 **Listen and underline what you hear.**

a. Prom is a (*school show / formal dance*).

b. It takes place at the end of the (*first / last*) year of High School after the exams.

c. (*Committees / the school staff*) discuss the theme, the place, the music and the DJs.

d. A Prom King and Queen are elected for their appearance and (*popularity / school results*).

e. Some students hire a (*Hummer / limo*) to get to the Prom.

f. Girls may spend (*hundreds / thousands*) of dollars on their dresses and shoes.

6 **Read the document and complete the stickers with the underlined words.**

On prom night, girls spend hours getting dressed together. They often wear long <u>evening dresses</u> and high-heeled shoes. Boys wear suits or <u>tuxedos</u> with a floral decoration called a <u>boutonniere</u> and a <u>bow tie</u>. They usually buy their dates* a <u>corsage</u>, which is a flower bracelet that goes on the girl's wrist.

* rendez-vous, « rencard »

Comment comprendre une vidéo

FICHE AP 1

Méthode

1 Acceptez de ne pas tout comprendre !

Essayez de saisir l'essentiel du message.

2 Repérez la thématique de la vidéo.

Observez la source et/ou la première image.

3 Lisez bien le titre de la vidéo.

Essayez de mobiliser le vocabulaire que vous connaissez déjà et qui correspond à la thématique de la vidéo.

4 Repérez les éléments visuels.

Utilisez vos connaissances pour situer le lieu de l'action et le contexte.

5 Repérez le nombre d'interlocuteurs.

Essayez de comprendre leurs liens et leurs relations.

6 Repérez les noms propres.

S'agit-il de noms de personnes, de villes, de lieux… ?

7 Repérez les indications chiffrées.

Essayez d'en comprendre le lien avec la vidéo.

8 Repérez les noms communs.

Repérez ceux qui vous semblent importants puis essayez de les mettre en relation.

9 Formulez des hypothèses.

Appuyez-vous sur ce que vous avez compris.

vidéo
50 Largest Cities of the United States of America - 6'30''
foucherconnect.fr/18tten39

Vos outils

audio
foucherconnect.fr/18tten07

A L'analyse visuelle

The elements make me think that…
Les éléments me laissent penser que…
The title seems to indicate that…
Le titre semble indiquer que…
The scene takes place in… *Le lieu de l'action est…*
The source of the document is…
La source du document est…

B L'expression d'hypothèses

I suppose that… *Je suppose que…*
To my mind/according to me… *Selon moi…*
I think that… *Je pense que…*
From what I can see… *D'après ce que je vois…*

● Lisez les conseils et coloriez les pictogrammes selon qu'il s'agit de regarder la vidéo et/ou de l'écouter.

FICHE AP 1 Comment comprendre une vidéo

Entraînez-vous !

Activité 1 Anticiper le contenu d'une vidéo à partir de son titre et d'une image

 # vidéo
10 Best Things in New York City (Honest Guide) – 5'19''
foucherconnect.fr/18tten08

A. Formulez deux hypothèses sur la thématique de la vidéo.

B. Citez les éléments visuels vous permettant de situer le lieu de l'action.

C. Citez les mots anglais que vous pouvez imaginer entendre dans cette vidéo.

D. Regardez la vidéo et vérifiez vos hypothèses.

Activité 2 Repérer les éléments significatifs d'une vidéo

 # vidéo
The Best Places to See in Santa Barbara – 2'34''
foucherconnect.fr/18tten09

A. Repérez le nombre d'interlocuteurs.

B. Citez les noms propres entendus.

C. Dites à quoi correspondent ces noms propres.

D. Repérez les noms communs expliquant les activités possibles dans cette ville.

E. Expliquez en français ce que vous avez compris de la vidéo en vous aidant des éléments précédents.

UNIT 3

TÂCHE FINALE Créer un audioguide pour la visite d'une ville

EOC – A2+

Welcome to London Tours

1 **Write the words on the corresponding labels.**

a river tour – a walking tour – a cycling tour – an open-top sightseeing bus[1] tour

1. bus touristique à impériale

2 1 Track 22 **Listen and complete.**

	Price	Length[2]
A river tour	....	....
A walking tour	....	At your own pace[3]
A cycling tour	....	....
A bus tour	....	....

2. durée ; 3. à votre rythme

BREAK IN VIDEO

 # vidéo
Big Bus Tours London
– 2'07''
foucherconnect.fr/18tten10

a. The video is about:
- ☐ a London bus tour
- ☐ a London river tour

b. The attractions mentioned are:
- ☐ Tower Bridge
- ☐ the London Eye
- ☐ Big Ben
- ☐ St Paul's Cathedral
- ☐ Buckingham Palace
- ☐ The Globe
- ☐ the Shard
- ☐ Tower of London

c. The tour ticket is valid for:
- ☐ 12 hours
- ☐ 24 hours

Famous Landmarks

Activity A Tower of London

1 Track 23 **Listen to the audio guide and underline the right information about the Tower of London.**

a. It is (situated / located) on the (East / South / North) Bank of the River Thames, (next to / near / opposite) Tower Bridge.

b. It was (created / built) by William the Conqueror.

c. It was used as (a palace / a prison / a museum / a theatre / a fortress).

d. It opens at (8:00 / 9:00 / 9:30) and a ticket is (£13.50 / £15.50 / £16.50).

2 Track 24 **Match the pictures and the captions. Then listen and check.**

1 Instruments of torture 2 The ravens 3 The Crown Jewels 4 Henry VIII's armour 5 The Yeomen Warders

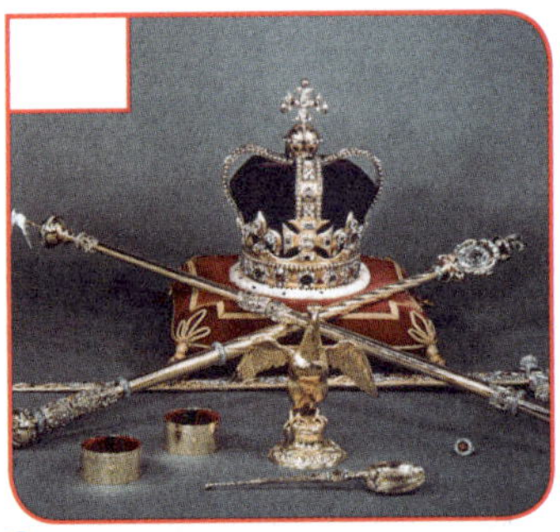

a.

b.

c.

d.

e.

Activity B A Unique Bridge

3 Track 25 **Complete the questions, then listen and check.**

Questions	Answers
a. .... is it situated?	Close to the Tower of London
b. .... was it built?	Between 1886 and 1894
c. .... can you see?	Panoramic views from the walkways*
d. .... can you visit?	A museum
e. .... is a ticket?	Adult £8.30 - Children £3.70
f. .... time does it open?	9:30 am

Tower Bridge

* *passerelles*

4 **Work in pairs. Use the elements above to make a dialogue about Tower Bridge.**

Activity C Buckingham Palace: The Queen's Official Home

Type of building >	a palace
Location >	in the borough* of Westminster
Date of construction >	1703 (for the Duke of Buckingham's wife)
Number of rooms >	775 (including a cinema, a swimming pool, a post office and a police station)
Visit / opening times >	only in the summer: daily / 9.30 am – 7.30 pm
What to see >	- the State Rooms (used for ceremonies) - the Queen's Gallery (paintings by Canaletto, Rembrandt, Rubens…) - the gardens (30 species of birds, 350 different flowers)
Number of visitors >	more than 400,000 each year

* *district*

5 1 Track 26 **Listen to the questions and write the answers. Then check your answers with your neighbour.**

a. ....
....

b. ....

c. ....
....

d. ....

e. ....

6 **Complete the questions. Then answer them orally.**

a. .... can you see in the Queen's gallery?
b. .... does it open for visits?
c. .... can you see 30 species of birds?
d. .... visitors are there each year?

FOCUS

a. **775 rooms = seven hundred and seventy-five rooms.**
b. **400,000 visitors = four hundred thousand visitors.**

- *Comment dit-on : cent :* ....
  mille : ....
- *Les milliers sont séparés des centaines par :* ....
- *J'ajoute* .... *entre les centaines et les dizaines.*
- *« **En 1703** » se dit :* ☐ *In seventeen o three* ☐ *In one thousand seven hundred and three*
- ***Huit livres trente** s'écrit :* ☐ *£8,30* ☐ *£8.30*
  et se dit : ☐ *eight pounds thirty* ☐ *eight thirty pounds*

Training ex. 2, 4

NOW ACT

7 **Work in pairs.** Ask and answer questions about famous landmarks.

Student A	**Student B**
Step 1 Go to **page 129** and ask **Student B** questions to complete the form.	**Step 1** Go to **page 130** and answer **Student A**'s questions.
Step 2 Then answer **Student B**'s questions.	**Step 2** Ask **Student A** questions to complete the form.

The Palace of Westminster

Activity D UK Political System

THE HOUSES OF PARLIAMENT

The UK Government sits in the Palace of Westminster or Houses of Parliament. It is situated on the north bank of the River Thames, in the centre of London. It was destroyed by fire in 1834 and was rebuilt between 1840 and 1870.

Parliament is the British legislative body. It's role is to decide laws[1], make decisions and check[2] that the government is running[3] the country properly. The Prime Minister leads the government and appoints Ministers to form the Cabinet.

1. THE QUEEN

She is the official Head of State. She "opens" Parliament each year and laws are passed in her name, but she only rules symbolically.

3. HOUSE OF LORDS

The House of Lords is made up of 675 members (called "peers"). They help make new laws.

2. HOUSE OF COMMONS

It is made up of 650 members of Parliament (MPs) who are elected by popular vote every five years. It is the real governing body of the UK. The House of Commons:
- proposes and passes new laws;
- authorizes taxes and controls the government's finances;
- debates current political issues[4].

1. lois ; 2. vérifier ; 3. diriger ; 4. questions

1 Read the document.

a. Circle the name of the building where Parliament meets.
b. Underline the names of the two Houses of Parliament.

2 Read the document again and answer the questions.

a. What is the document about? ....
....
b. What is the role of Parliament? ....
....
....

3 Find in the document the English for:

a. *nomme* (§0) : ....
b. *les lois sont adoptées* (§1) : ....
c. *gouverne* (§1) : ....
d. *est composé de* (§3) : ....

4 Write "True" (T) or "False" (F)

a. The Queen governs the country. (....)
b. The Prime Minister is the head of government. (....)
c. Peers are members of the House of Commons. (....)
d. The House of Commons makes laws. (....)

FOCUS

a. It was destroyed in 1834.
b. MPs are elected by popular vote.

- *Soulignez les formes verbales.*
- *Complétez :*

- Phrase **a** *: .... au .... + participe passé du verbe*
- Phrase **b** *: .... au .... + participe passé du verbe.*
Il s'agit de la forme : ☐ *active* ☐ *passive*

Training ex. 5

NOW ACT

5 Explain in French the British political system.

VIDEO TIME 3

At the Tower of London

 # vidéo
Moira Cameron, the first Yeoman Warder at the Tower of London – 2'55''
foucherconnect.fr/18tten11

Step 1 Before watching the video.

1 **Read the title and look at the picture above. Then make hypotheses about the topic of the video.**

....

....

....

....

....

....

....

....

Step 2 Watch the whole video.

2 **Tick the correct information.**

a. The video is about:
- ☐ a woman working at London Bridge
- ☐ a woman working at the Tower of London

b. She is:
- ☐ the first female Yeoman Warder
- ☐ the third female Yeoman Warder

c. Yeomen Warders:
- ☐ are the guardians of the Tower
- ☐ look after the visitors
- ☐ wear green and black uniforms

Step 3 Watch the video up to 0:44.

3 **Underline the right information.**

To become a Yeoman Warder:

a. You must be retired (*parliamentary / military*) personnel.

b. You must have spent (*22 / 24 / 26*) years in Her Majesty's Armed Forces.

c. You have to have a good conduct (*award / reward / medal*).

d. You have to be Warrant Officer class (*1 / 2*).

Step 4 Watch the video from 0:45 to 1:10.

4 **Circle the words you hear.**

"There was an (*advertisement / article*) in the Soldier (*revue / magazine*) and it said that it wasn't just a job for the (*girls / boys*). So, I (*asked / applied*) for it, because I just thought it was a really (*interesting / motivating*) job".

HELP!

apply for poser sa candidature à
look after s'occuper de
posting affectation
retired retraité
Warrant Officer Class 1 adjudant
Warrant Officer Class 2 sous-officier
EIIR Queen Elizabeth II (R is for *Regina* = Queen)

Fiche **VIDEO TIME 3** *At the Tower of London* **complète disponible en téléchargement**

UNIT 3

Training

exo foucherconnect.fr/18tten12

IN TUNE

A 1 Track 27 **Écoutez et répétez les nombres suivants.**

£15.55 – 17 – 70 – $398 – 7,942 – €777.30 – 25,829

B 1 Track 28 **Entourez les nombres que vous entendez, puis prononcez-les.**

a. 16 – 60
b. £13.50 – £30.50
c. 982 - 962
d. $275.50 – $275.15
e. 316 – 3,016
f. €4,570- €4,517

1 **À l'aide des descriptions, complétez la grille avec le nom des attractions pour découvrir le mot caché.**

1. The biggest Ferris wheel in Europe. You can have a great view of London from here.
2. It is the official home of the Queen of England.
3. It is 244 metres long. Boats can pass under it.
4. It is an old castle. It was also a prison.
5. Ministers meet there to speak about politics.

2 **Écrivez ce que vous lisez en toutes lettres.**

a. 976: ....
b. in 1975: ....
c. £3,824: ....
....
d. $53.80: ....
e. in 2012: ....
....

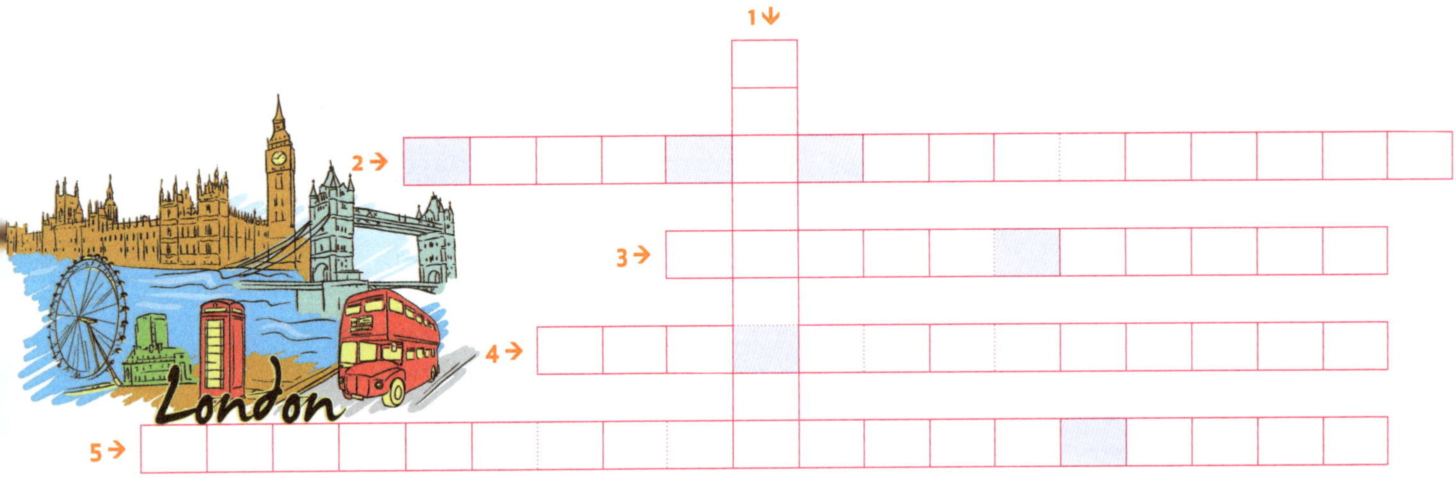

Le mot caché est : ....

Vocabulary

Nouns
a bank une rive
a bridge un pont
a bus tour une visite en bus
a cycling tour une visite à vélo
a landmark un monument
opening times horaires d'ouverture
an open-top sightseeing bus un bus touristique à impériale
a raven un corbeau
a river tour une visite en bateau
a walking tour une visite à pied

Verbs
build* construire
cross traverser
rule gouverner
run* diriger (un pays)

Adjectives
situated/located situé

Adverbs
daily tous les jours
symbolically symboliquement

3 Écrivez les horaires suivants en toutes lettres puis lisez-les à haute voix.

a b c d e

a. ....

b. ....

c. ....

d. ....

e. ....

4 1 Track 29 **Écoutez et complétez.**

a. The museum opens at .... every day.

b. It costs £ ....

c. It was built in ....

d. There are .... visitors every year.

5 **Donnez des informations sur le Tower Bridge à l'aide des éléments ci-dessous. Utilisez la forme passive au présent.**

a. Tower Bridge / situate / on the River Thames

....

b. The bridge / paint / white and blue

....

c. The towers / use / as a museum

....

d. Tower Bridge / visit / by more than 380,000 tourists every year

....

....

e. Tower Bridge / cross / by over 40,000 people every day

....

....

Language TIPS

Les nombres

→ 4,915 → four **thousand** nine **hundred** and fifteen.

→ 364 → three hundred **and** sixty-four.

Les prix

À l'écrit → £15.60

À l'oral → 'fifteen **pounds** sixty'.

Les dates (années)

1967 → nineteen sixty-seven.

2015 → twenty fifteen *ou* two thousand and fifteen.

La forme passive

→ **be** *conjugué* + *participe passé du verbe*

The castle **was built** in 1836.

Le château a été construit en 1836.

It **is visited** by many tourists every year.

Il est visité par de nombreux touristes chaque année.

FINAL TASK 3 Create an Audioguide for a Bus Tour

SCENARIO Pour préparer un voyage scolaire à Londres, vous devez créer un audioguide présentant un ou deux sites touristiques pour la visite en bus de la ville.

1. Royal Albert Hall
2. London Eye
3. British Museum
4. St Paul's Cathedral
5. The Globe
6. The Shard
7. Hyde Park
8. Borough Market
9. Madame Tussaud's
10. 10, Downing Street
11. Trafalgar Square
12. Piccadilly Circus
13. Harrods
14. Hamleys

Étape 1 Trouver des informations pertinentes sur un site touristique CE – A2+

- Choisissez un ou deux sites touristiques de Londres dont vous aimeriez parler (vous pouvez vous aider du plan ci-dessus).
- Pour chaque site, cherchez les informations pour compléter la fiche ci-dessous.

Name of the attraction:	
Location (part of London)	....
Type of attraction	☐museum ☐church ☐park ☐market ☐palace ☐building ☐other: ....
Date of opening / building	....
What to see / What to do	....
Opening times	....
Ticket price	☐adults: .... ☐students: .... ☐free
Other information	

Étape 2 Présenter un site touristique EOC – A2+

- Utilisez votre fiche pour vous entraîner à présenter oralement les sites que vous avez choisis à la manière d'un audioguide.
- Enregistrez votre présentation orale.

mon bilan UNIT 3

	J'ai réussi à...	– –	–	+	++
EOI	Demander ou donner des informations sur un site touristique				
CE	Comprendre un article sur le système politique britannique				
CO	Comprendre un reportage sur la Tour de Londres				
EO	Présenter un site touristique de Londres				

UNIT 3

S'inspirer d'un modèle connu

CCF PREP 5

PARTIE 1 EOC

LET'S TRAIN!

1 Track 30 **Écoutez l'audioguide sur Tower Bridge et complétez le script.**

2 Track 30 **Écoutez à nouveau. Indiquez les pauses par un slash (/).**

.... **Tower Bridge!**

Tower Bridge is a suspension .... over the River Thames .... near the Tower of London, and that is why Tower Bridge .... Tower Bridge! Now, ... about the history of Tower Bridge. .... started in 1886 and it took eight years to complete. It .... officially .... in 1894 by the Prince of Wales. ...., Tower Bridge consists of two towers joined by two walkways for pedestrians and, at the lower level, by the road bridge for motor traffic. You .... along the walkways, which give stunning .... of the Thames and many famous London .... You can also .... the museum to see how Tower Bridge ....

.... your visit!

3 Track 30 **Écoutez à nouveau et entraînez-vous à lire l'extrait à haute voix en reproduisant le modèle (intonation, prononciation, pauses).**

YOUR TURN!

4 **En vous inspirant du modèle d'audioguide ci-dessus, utilisez les informations données pour enregistrer la présentation de Central Park.**

- **Landmark:** Central Park / the most visited urban park in the USA
- **Location:** Manhattan / New York City (in the centre)
- **First opened to the public:** 1854
- **What to see:** artificial lakes / large woods / beautiful sculptures
- **What to do:**
  - cycle / hang out in the park
  - in the summer / open-air theatre with famous actors

5 **Choisissez un lieu que vous aimez dans votre ville ou que vous avez aimé lors d'un voyage et présentez-le en suivant le même modèle.**

CCF PREP 6

PARTIE 2 EOI

Répondre à des questions pour présenter un musée

LET'S TRAIN!

1. *Jack l'éventreur* ; 2. meurtres

1 1 Track 31 À l'aide du document, répondez aux questions enregistrées.

a. ....

b. ....

c. ....

d. ....

e. ....

2 À l'oral, posez deux questions supplémentaires sur ce musée.

YOUR TURN!

Welcome to 48 Doughty Street, the London home of Charles Dickens, one of the world's greatest storytellers

- Discover the Dickens family home.
- Explore his study and see Dickens' desk.
- Buy exclusive gifts from our shop (books, mugs, posters, pens...).
- Visit our garden Café for a delicious drink

Tuesday to Sunday 10am – 5pm
(last admission at 4 pm)
Adult: £9.00
Child (6-16 years): £4

3 Préparez cinq questions à poser à votre partenaire sur le musée Charles Dickens. Puis répondez aux siennes.

UNIT **4**

TÂCHE FINALE → **Réaliser une fiche-conseil sur un lieu de stage** — **EE – A2+**

Ready for Work

Mr Jackson is a …………………………. He supervises Tracy and gives her ………………………….

Tracy is a ……………………. She is doing a two-week ……………………………… in a clothes shop.

She's very happy with her ……………………………… She has a two-hour …………………………….

1 1 Track 32 **Listen and fill in the information you hear about Tracy.**

Age: …… **School:** Vocational ……………………
Location: Sunderland / ……………………………… of England / …………………………… Newcastle.
Occupation: …………………………………………… of a BTEC National Diploma.

2 1 Track 32 **Listen again and fill in the labels with the following elements.**

trainee – tutor – lunch break – work placement – advice[1] – schedule

3 **Match the equivalents.**

a trainee	○	○	*les horaires*
a schedule	○	○	*une pause déjeuner*
a work placement	○	○	*un(e) stagiaire*
a tutor	○	○	*un(e) tuteur(trice)*
BTEC National Diploma	○	○	*un stage*
a lunch break	○	○	*un baccalauréat professionnel*

BREAK IN VIDEO

 # vidéo How to Prepare for Work Experience - 1'46''
foucherconnect.fr/18tten13

a. **The video is about tips[1] to help you to:**
☐ find a work placement
☐ introduce yourself at a work placement

b. **With work experience, you can gain:**
☐ confidence ☐ skills

c. **Number the tips.**
Tip ………: write an introductory pitch.
Tip ………: plan in advance.
Tip ………: give yourself a goal.

1. *conseils*

First Day at Work

Activity A Get Ready!

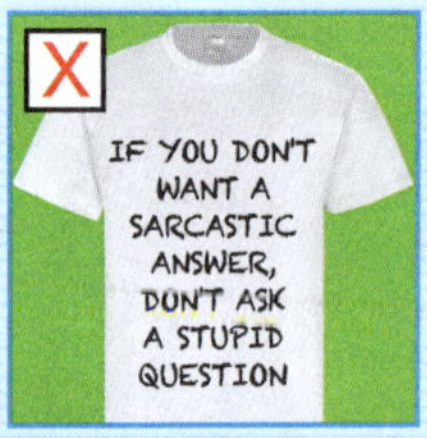

1 **Complete the labels with the corresponding words.**
a collared shirt – a neat haircut – a printed T-shirt – sneakers – clean and appropriate shoes – dirty and wrinkled clothes

2 1 Track 33 **Listen and complete with *should, shouldn't, 'd better* and *'d better not.***

a. You .... wear dirty and wrinkled clothes.
b. You .... wear a collared shirt.
c. You .... wear sneakers.
d. You .... have a neat haircut.

FOCUS

a. You 'd better wear a shirt.
b. You should have a neat haircut.
c. You'd better not forget to greet your co-workers.
d. You shouldn't cross your arms.

- *Quelle expression soulignée signifie :*
- *« Tu ferais bien/mieux de » :* ....
- *« Tu devrais » :* ....

- *Ces expressions expriment :*
☐ *un ordre* ☐ *un conseil* ☐ *une obligation*

Training ex. 1, 2

Activity B How to behave[1]

3 1 Track 34 **Listen and tick G for the good behaviours[2] and B for the bad ones.**

a. greet your co-workers	G ☐	B ☐
b. be polite	G ☐	B ☐
c. speak clearly	G ☐	B ☐
d. cross your arms	G ☐	B ☐
e. chew gum	G ☐	B ☐
f. take notes	G ☐	B ☐
g. turn off your mobile	G ☐	B ☐

4 **Use the information above to give advice to a new trainee.**

1. *se comporter* ; 2. *attitudes*

Activity C Skills and Qualities

a.	b.	c.	d. ....
You need to be creative. You also have to be .... at recognising flavours and ingredients. As you work in a team, it is important to be .... and	You should be .... at appointments with customers. You have to be .... and .... about the products that you're selling. You need to be good at negotiating.	You need to be .... in fixing and repairing things. You have to be good at solving problems quickly and not be afraid to get dirty. And of course, you need to be .... about cars!	You need to be .... with patients. It's essential to be .... and .... to any changes in a patient's health. You have to be .... — you can be called any time!

5 **Write the jobs under the corresponding pictures.**

a car mechanic – a nurse – a sales representative – a chef

6 1 Track 35 **Listen to the job descriptions and complete with the adjectives below.**

attentive – caring – cheerful – cooperative – flexible – enthusiastic – organised – passionate – punctual – qualified – responsible – skilled

7 **Look at the photos and say what qualities and skills you need for these jobs.**

a. To work as a salesperson, you ....
....
....

b. To work as a waitress, you ....
....
....

a salesperson

a waitress

NOW ACT

8 **Go to page 127 and look at the pictures. Give advice to these trainees for their first work placement.**

FOCUS

a. You **have to be** flexible.
b. You **need to be** punctual.

- *Ces deux énoncés expriment :*

☐ *ce qu'il est possible de faire*
☐ *ce qu'il faut faire*

Training ex. 4

Placement Preparation

Activity D Work Placement Guidelines

WHAT TO DO IF ...

You are going to be late for work
This shouldn't happen. However, if something happens to make you late you should phone your tutor at the workplace to tell him/her you are on your way. He/she should understand, provided that you get there as soon as possible, and your reason is genuine[1] and unavoidable[2]. However, do not make a habit of this!

You are unwell and cannot go to work
Phone your tutor before your normal starting time and explain why and how long you will be absent. Ask if they require a doctor's certificate. Your parents should also phone your school.

You are injured at work
Even if you think the injury is not important, you should report it to your employer immediately. There are specific procedures for your employer to follow.

You feel you are being harassed at work
It is essential, if you are not comfortable with your workmates or tutor, for you to discuss this with someone immediately. It can be someone from your family or from school. Do not wait until the placement is over. It is important to resolve the problem as soon as possible. If necessary the school may need to act on your behalf.

1. *réelle/vraie* ; 2. *inévitable*

1 Read the document and explain what the document is about.

....

....

....

....

2 Find in the document the English for:+

a. *être en retard (§1):* ....
b. *à condition que (§1):* ....
c. *malade (§2):* ....
d. *blessé(e) (§3) :* ....
e. *harcelé(e) (§4):* ....
f. *collègues (§4):* ....
g. *résoudre (§4):* ....
h. *à votre place/en votre nom (§4) :* ....

3 "Right" or "Wrong"?

	Right	Wrong
a. If you are unwell, you only need to inform your tutor.	☐	☐
b. If you feel uncomfortable at work, wait until the end of the placement to discuss it.	☐	☐
c. The school can solve the problem for you.	☐	☐

4 Answer the questions.

a. What do you need to do to be excused for your lateness?

....

....

b. When do you have to phone your tutor if you are unwell?

....

....

c. Why should you report your injury immediately?

....

....

d. Who can you discuss it with if you feel harassed at work?

....

....

NOW ACT

5 Say in French what you have to do in the four situations mentioned in the document.

TÂCHE 3 **Comprendre les avantages d'une expérience professionnelle**

CO – A2+

VIDEO TIME 4

How to Get Work Experience

 # vidéo
How to Help Your Teenager Get the Best Out of Work Experience – 2'13''
foucherconnect.fr/18tten14

Step 1 **Before watching the video.**

1 Read the title and look at the picture above. Who is this video aimed at?

....

....

Step 2 **Watch the whole video.**

2 Tick the correct information.

a. Teenagers tell about the: ☐ benefits ☐ disadvantages of doing work experience.

b. They advise parents:
☐ to help their children to find a work placement
☐ to let their children find a work placement by themselves

c. ☐ There is only one way
☐ There are different ways
for teenagers to have work experience.

Step 3 **Watch the video up to 0:32.**

3 Circle the words you hear.

"(*Work experience / placement*) is a great way for us to (*spare / spend*) time out of the (*school / classroom*) learning about the (*world of work / day of work*) and it can help us with our future career (*choices / decisions*)."

Step 4 **Watch the video from 0:33 to 0:46.**

4 Answer the questions.

a. How many days of work experience do you need to get the diploma?

....

b. What do many schools now offer to get work experience?

....

Step 5 **Watch the video from 0:47 to 1:10.**

5 Number the tips in the order you hear them.

To help their children, parents can…

(......) Get in touch with the school.
(......) Talk to a careers advisor.
(......) Ask them what their passions are.
(......) Go to a local Connexions office.

HELP!

apprenticeship un apprentissage
a career une carrière
a careers advisor un(e) conseiller(ère) d'orientation
a library une bibliothèque
prospects des perspectives
a voluntary job un travail bénévole

Fiche VIDEO TIME 4 *How to Help Your Teenager…* **complète disponible en téléchargement**

UNIT 4

Training

#exo foucherconnect.fr/18tten15

IN TUNE

A 1 Track 36 **Écoutez la prononciation des lettres « sh » et « ch », puis répétez les mots.**

should – shirt – chew – cheerful

B 1 Track 37 **Classez les mots suivants en fonction de la prononciation des lettres « sh » et « ch ». Écoutez et vérifiez.**

check – shirt – shoes – choose – change – China – show-off – shape

/ʃ/ should	/tʃ/ chew

1 **Complétez les phrases à l'aide de *should / shouldn't / 'd better/ 'd better not* en vous aidant des images. Utilisez les verbes suivants.**

ask – be – dress – wear (x2) – switch off – keep

For your first day:

a. You .... sunglasses.

b. You .... your mobile phone.

c. You .... there on time.

d. You .... baggy jeans.

e. You .... your earphones in.

f. You .... questions if you don't know something.

2 **Donnez des conseils pour les situations suivantes.**

a. I can't get up in the morning and I always arrive late at work.

I think you... ....

....

b. I don't know how to get to my workplace.

....

c. I don't know my tutor's name.

....

d. I feel very nervous about my first day tomorrow.

....

a

b

c

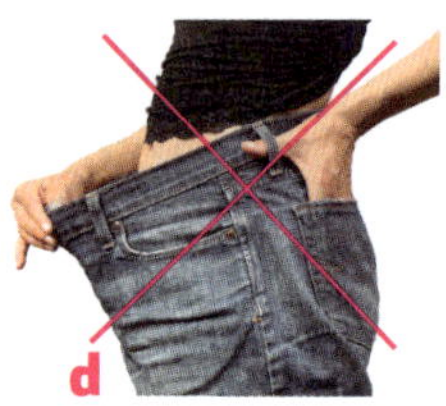
d

e

f

Vocabulary

Nouns

BTEC National Diploma Baccalauréat professionnel
a schedule un emploi du temps / des horaires
skills des compétences
sneakers des baskets
a trainee un stagiaire
a tutor un(e) tuteur(trice)
a vocational school un lycée professionnel
a work placement un stage

Verbs

be* on time être à l'heure
keep* garder/conserver
switch off éteindre
take* exercise faire de l'exercice
wear* porter (un vêtement)

Adjectives

caring attentionné
cheerful enjoué/joyeux
cooperative coopératif
creative créatif
enthusiastic enthousiaste, passionné
flexible flexible, souple
passionate passionné
punctual ponctuel
qualified qualifié

Adverbs

clearly clairement
properly correctement

3 Complétez la grille avec l'adjectif correspondant en vous aidant des définitions.

cheerful – cooperative – creative – flexible – passionate – punctual – qualified

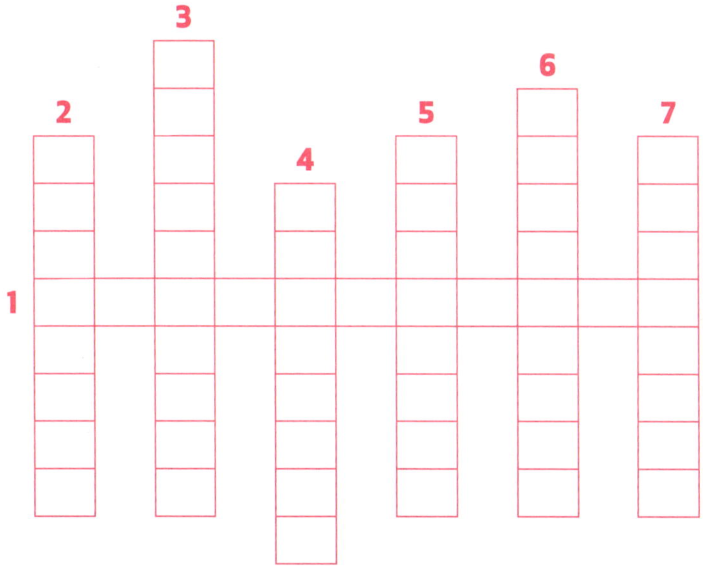

1. works well with others
2. always on time
3. fond of, crazy about something
4. can change easily
5. makes and invents new things
6. has experience and skills
7. is always pleasant and smiling

4 Entourez la forme verbale qui convient.

A To work as a secretary…

a. You (*don't need to* / *have to*) speak clearly on the phone.
b. You (*have to* / *don't need to*) be creative.
c. You (*need to* / *don't need to*) be polite.
d. You (*'d better* / *shouldn't*) wear sneakers.
e. You (*have to* / *don't need to*) be organised.

B To work as a firefighter…

a. You (*have to* / *shouldn't*) wear a uniform.
b. You (*need to* / *don't need to*) be courageous.
c. You (*don't need to* / *have to*) be good at repairing.
d. You (*'d better not* / *should*) take exercise to keep fit[1].
e. You (*need to* / *don't need to*) be cooperative.

1. *rester en forme*

Language TIPS

Le conseil

→ **should + V / shouldn't + V**

You should take notes.
Tu devrais prendre des notes.

You shouldn't wear sneakers.
Tu ne devrais pas porter de baskets.

→ **You'd better + V**
You'd better not + V

You'd better be polite.
Tu ferais mieux d'être poli.

La nécessité, l'obligation

→ **need to + V**

You need to be qualified.
Vous devez être qualifié.

→ **have to + V**

You have to be flexible.
Vous devez / il faut être flexible.

FINAL TASK 4 Write a Tip Sheet

SCENARIO

Dans le cadre de l'EGLS (enseignement général lié à la spécialité), vous devez rédiger une fiche de conseils à suivre par un futur stagiaire qui souhaiterait aller dans l'entreprise où vous venez d'effectuer votre premier stage de seconde.

Étape 1 Compléter une fiche à propos de son lieu de stage EE – A2+

- Trouvez les informations concernant l'entreprise où vous avez effectué votre stage pour compléter la fiche ci-dessous.

Business / company name	....
Address	....
Contact person / title (eg. manager)	....
Type of business /company	☐ supermarket ☐ insurance company ☐ (clothes /...) shop ☐ youth centre[1] ☐ town hall ☐ workshop ☐ other: ....
Working hours	Start: .... Finish: .... Flexible: ☐ yes ☐ no
Breaks	From: .... to: ....
Lunch arrangements	☐ packed lunch ☐ canteen ☐ break room ☐ restaurant ☐ other: ....
Clothing requirements	☐ casual ☐ formal ☐ uniform ☐ overalls[2] More details: ....

1. *MJC* ; **2.** *bleu de travail*

Étape 2 Réaliser une fiche de conseils EE – A2+

- Rédigez dix conseils ou recommandations à suivre sur ce lieu de stage. Vous les classerez par rubriques. (Exemple : « *Working Hours* », « *Lunch arrangements* », « *Clothing* », « *Attitude* », « *Qualities* »...)
- Vous pouvez insérer des photos (tenue, lieu...).
- Utilisez un logiciel de traitement de texte pour présenter votre fiche.

10 TIPS TO HELP YOU MAKE A GOOD IMPRESSION AT (Name / address / type of business or company)		
Column	☺	☹
1...		
2...		

mon bilan UNIT 4

	J'ai réussi à...	−−	−	+	++
EOC	Donner des conseils, des recommandations				
CE	Comprendre des recommandations pour bien débuter un stage				
CO	Comprendre les avantages d'une expérience professionnelle				
EE	Réaliser une fiche de conseils				

UNIT 4

Utiliser des mots outils pour justifier un choix

CCF PREP 7

PARTIE 1 EOC

LET'S TRAIN!

1 Track 38 **Écoutez et soulignez ce que vous entendez. Puis répétez.**

a. I'd like to do my work placement in a garage (*because / because of*) I'm fond of mechanics.

b. I'm very communicative and I love meeting people, (*because / that's why*) I want to become a sales representative.

c. I want to go on a work placement (*to / in order to*) gain new professional skills.

d. I really enjoy talking to people and I'm very organised, (*so / that's why*) I believe I can be a good secretary.

e. I've chosen this work place (*in order to / because of*) my passion for cosmetics.

f. I'm doing a BTEC national in catering (*to / in order to*) work in a hotel.

2 **Reliez les mots de liaison à leur traduction.**

a. because ○	○ *c'est pourquoi*
b. because of ○	○ *afin de*
c. that's why ○	○ *à cause de*
d. to ○	○ *pour* (+V)
e. in order to ○	○ *parce que*

YOUR TURN!

3 **Vous avez choisi ce lieu de stage. À partir des informations suivantes, justifiez votre choix. Utilisez les mots de liaison de l'exercice 2.**

My choice: a big restaurant

My passions
- cooking
- preparing meals for my family

My qualities
- co-operative → work in a team
- creative → new recipes[1]

My expectations[2]
- gain new skills
- learn new things

1. *recettes* ; 2. *mes attentes*

CCF PREP 8

PARTIE 3 CE

Comprendre un article sur les codes vestimentaires

Dress Codes Around the World

Formal or casual[1]? That is the question pertaining[2] to business attire all over the world. Let's have a closer look.

Argentina

Very formal, almost conservative. Dark or neutral colours, especially for men. Women have to add a dash of style, with smart dresses and skirts, balancing business and trend.

Australia

The country where "smart casual" (unless you work in a very strict business environment) meets with "casual Friday". In other words, it's most unlikely for you to be required to wear a tie here.

China

If you're not Chinese, you will probably find a job in the financial/business sector, therefore you'll have to stick to the most conservative side of dressing. The mantra is "not to show off[3]" and remember to apply it to jewellery too. If you're a woman, you must remember that anything revealing can be labelled "inappropriate". Your dress hem[4] should always fall below the knee and a high neckline is strongly recommended.

Germany

This may come as a surprise, given the fact that —aside[5] from Berlin— Germany is not famous for its fashion sense, and definitely not laid back. Nevertheless, even though you have to look professional, you can choose your pattern, colours and shapes, especially when it comes to shirts and ties. But be careful! Though you'll be relatively free, the employers do have the right to enforce certain dress codes, e.g. women wearing bras to work.

www.injob.com.

1. *décontracté* ; 2. *concernant* ; 3. *se mettre en avant* ; 4. *ourlet* ; 5. *à part*

Répondez aux questions en français.

1. Quel est le sujet du document ?

....

....

2. Quelle tenue professionnelle faut-il adopter en Australie ?

....

....

3. Dans lequel des quatre pays cités la tenue est-elle la plus stricte ? Quelle est la règle de base dans ce pays ?

....

....

4. Quelles recommandations les Chinoises doivent-elles suivre ?

....

....

5. Les employés en Allemagne sont-ils entièrement libres de porter ce qu'ils veulent ?

....

....

American Billionaires

Culture CLICK 2

❶ .... D. Rockefeller (1839–.........)

The richest .... of all time: he decided to refine .... instead of drilling[1] it.

❷ **AN OIL INDUSTRY BUSINESSMAN**

Career: At ...., an assistant bookkeeper[2].
At ...., into a business partnership.
In ...., Rockefeller & Andrews.

Founder of the .... in 1870.

- He then controlled .... of all oil ....
- In 1916, he became the country's ....

A RELIGIOUS MAN AND A PATRON[3]

Donations: about $ .... to .... institutions and charities[4] for ...., public health, ... and the arts.

Foundings

- The .... + ... University
- The ....

1. forer ; 2. un comptable ; 3. un mécène ; 4. des œuvres caritatives

1 Track 39 **Listen and complete the information.**

2 Track 40 **Decide if the facts about Bill Gates are true or false. Listen and check.**

	True	False
a. Bill Gates is so rich that he throws $1,000 bills to the wind.	☐	☐
b. At Microsoft, Bill Gates used to memorize employees' license plates[1] to check their comings and goings.	☐	☐
c. Every time you forward an e-mail from the Lottery Bill Gates Foundation, you will receive hundreds of dollars.	☐	☐
d. Bill Gates' children will inherit only $10 million each — just a fraction of his $81.1 billion net worth[2].	☐	☐

1. une plaque d'immatriculation ; 2. valeur nette

Quiz

1 Bill Gates became a billionaire by the age of:
- a. 21 ☐
- b. 31 ☐
- c. 41 ☐

2 The world's richest woman is:
- a. Laurene Powell Jobs ☐
- b. Jacqueline Mars ☐
- c. Françoise Bettencourt-Meyers ☐

3 Steve Jobs made his first billion with:
- a. Apple ☐
- b. Next ☐
- c. Pixar ☐

4 Cornelius Vanderbilt built his wealth in:
- a. railroads and shipping ☐
- b. oil refining ☐
- c. the steel industry ☐

5 Billionaire Oprah Winfrey is known as:
- a. a talk-show host ☐
- b. a diplomat ☐
- c. a politician ☐

6 Evan Spiegel, the youngest American billionaire, is CEO of:
- a. Instagram ☐
- b. Snapchat ☐
- c. Facebook ☐

7 At 101 years old, America's oldest billionaire was:
- a. Andrew Carnegie ☐
- b. David Rockefeller ☐
- c. John Jacob Astor ☐

8 At McDonald's, Bill Gates and Warren Buffett can eat:
- a. for free with their gold cards ☐
- b. with Ronald Mc Donald ☐
- c. a burger called the billionaire ☐

9 At the rate of $1 million a day, Bill Gates' money would be spent:
- a. in 150 years ☐
- b. in 218 years ☐
- c. in 320 years ☐

10 The world's richest man is:
- a. Bill Gates ☐
- b. Mark Zuckerberg ☐
- c. Jeff Bezos ☐

1 Track 42 **Listen and check.**

Your score: ... /10

With an estimated $38.4 billion, Alice Walton, the heiress[1] to the Walmart[2] fortune, is the richest woman in the US. However, Alice has never taken an active role running Walmart and has instead become a patron of the arts. When she was 10, she bought her first work of art: a reproduction of a Picasso painting for $2. In 2011, she opened a museum called Crystal Bridges to house her private art collection, presenting original works from legendary American artists such as Andy Warhol, Norman Rockwell and Georgia O'Keefe. Today her collection is worth $500 million.

1. *une héritière* ; 2. *multinationale spécialisée dans la grande distribution*

3 Read the document and answer the questions.

a. Who is the richest woman in the US?

....

b. How much money does her fortune represent? ....

c. What is she interested in? ....

d. What is Crystal Bridges?

....

e. How much money is her collection worth? ....

4 1 Track 41 **Listen and select the information you hear.**

a. The film depicts the life of (Richard Branson / Howard Hughes) from 1927 to 1947. He was an American businessman who became a (film producer / actor) and who was very influential in the (oil / aviation) industry.

b. He was one of the most financially successful individuals in the (world / USA).

c. After producing big-budget movies, he employed many engineers in his (aircraft company / studio).

d. In the '30s and '40s, he set multiple world air speed records. He (purchased / created) TWA, an airline company, and worked for the Army Air Forces.

e. In 1946, he was (severely injured / killed) when his plane crashed during a test flight.

f. He suffered from obsessive-compulsive disorder and became more and more (paranoid / shy).

Comment mémoriser du vocabulaire

FICHE AP 2

Méthode

1 Regardez des vidéos ou écoutez des enregistrements sonores.

Écoutez ou regardez les mêmes documents plusieurs fois afin de mieux mémoriser le vocabulaire entendu. Après l'écoute, répétez à haute voix ce que vous avez compris.

2 Parlez.

Profitez de toutes les occasions pour parler anglais et ainsi mémoriser le vocabulaire nouveau.

3 Lisez des documents écrits ou visitez des sites en ligne.

Lisez des articles dans des magazines ou en ligne sur des sujets qui vous intéressent.

4 Utilisez un dictionnaire bilingue. (A)

Cela vous permettra de vérifier ou découvrir le sens et la prononciation des mots. Lisez les mots à haute voix, répétez leur prononciation plusieurs fois afin de bien les mémoriser.

5 Faites des listes de mots que vous noterez dans un carnet et/ou enregistrez-les. (B)

Regroupez les mots par thème avec leur traduction. Relisez ou réécoutez souvent ces mots (une à deux fois par semaine si possible).

6 Utilisez les mots nouveaux lors d'une conversation.

Essayez d'utiliser 3 à 6 mots ou expressions que vous venez de mémoriser.

7 Entrainez-vous à écrire en anglais.

Choisissez un sujet qui vous intéresse (vie personnelle, actualité…) et écrivez quelques lignes en utilisant des mots nouveaux.

8 Pratiquez l'anglais tous les jours.

Il suffit de 10 à 15 minutes d'anglais tous les jours pour bien mémoriser.

Vos outils

sites foucherconnect.fr/18tten16

A Des dictionnaires bilingues en ligne
www.wordreference.com/enfr
www.larousse.fr/dictionnaires/anglais-francais
dictionary.cambridge.org/fr

B Des services convertissant tout texte en fichier audio
www.fromtexttospeech.com
www.naturalreaders.com/index.html
acapela-box.com

● Commencez votre carnet de vocabulaire et/ou fichier audio.
Organisez-le par thèmes (sport, voyages, nourriture, professionnel, films, chansons…) en laissant de la place pour des thèmes futurs. Écrivez et/ou enregistrez des mots nouveaux.
Illustrez votre carnet si vous le souhaitez.

FICHE AP 2

Comment mémoriser du vocabulaire

Entraînez-vous !

Activité 1 Mémoriser à partir d'une vidéo

Google Glass How-to

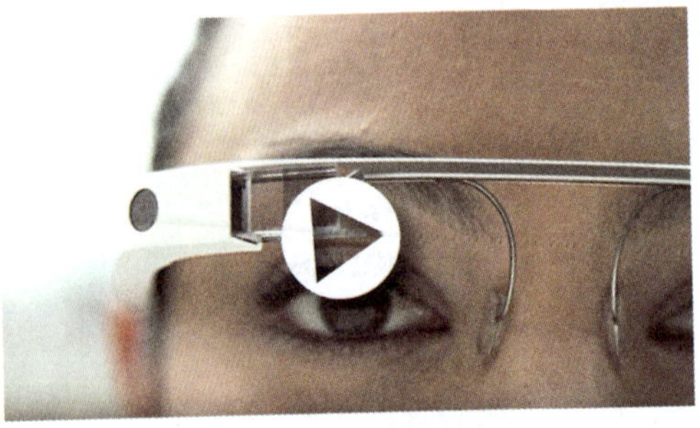

 # vidéo
Google Glass How-to
– 1'07''
foucherconnect.fr/18tten17

A. **Regardez la vidéo plusieurs fois (avec sous-titres si besoin).**
Notez ci-dessous pour chaque partie les mots nouveaux sans noter toute la phrase entendue.

a. Basics: ....

b. Your touchpad: ....

c. Adjust the display: ....

d. Your timeline: ....

e. See more: ....

B. **Entraînez-vous à expliquer oralement ce que vous avez compris.**
Pour chaque partie, dites au moins une phrase en utilisant les mots nouveaux que vous avez notés.

C. **Notez les mots nouveaux dans votre carnet de vocabulaire et/ou enregistrez-les dans vos fichiers audio.**

Activité 2 Mémoriser à partir d'un texte

The Hidden Dangers of Too Much Screen Time

From cell phones and tablets to televisions and laptops, glowing screens make our lives much more convenient and more entertaining. Yet excessive screen time (more than four hours per day) has been linked to problems with heart, vision, sleep and obesity.
And studies have found that excessive media exposure in kids may contribute to attention problems, difficulties in school, sleep issues and eating disorders.
Here are simple strategies that can help reduce exposure.
Don't keep your phone near your bed at night. This will help you resist the temptation to look at it as soon as you wake up.
Find healthier hobbies. Enjoy family time. Meet friends. Stimulate your mind with board games. Challenge your endurance on a run or a swim. Read books or magazines (printed on paper).
Enjoy everything in moderation. Simply establish rules and guidelines. Want to watch your favourite show on Thursday night? Go for it! But limit yourself to one hour.

A. **Lisez l'article en essayant de bien comprendre le sens général. Échangez avec votre voisin sur ce que chacun a compris.**

B. **Relisez en surlignant les mots nouveaux :**

- en vert, ceux que vous ne connaissiez pas mais dont vous devinez le sens (exemple : *excessive*) ;
- en jaune, ceux dont vous ne comprenez pas le sens.

C. **Utilisez un dictionnaire et/ou les outils en ligne pour comprendre le sens de mots inconnus et en vérifier la prononciation.**

D. **Répétez tous les mots nouveaux. Notez-les et/ou enregistrez-les.**

UNIT
5

TÂCHE FINALE **Réaliser un jeu de *Jeopardy***

EE – A2+

Fabulous India

1. The Indian ....

Three horizontal bands of colour:
- saffron[1] for .... and sacrifice;
- white for truth and ....;
- green for faith and ....;
- and a wheel of life[2] in the ....

2. A land of ....

Most Indians live on less than .... a day, but a million Indians are ....

3. The most admired .... in the world: the Taj Mahal

In 1638, Mogul Emperor Shah Jahan began the building of a magnificent .... in memory of his ....

1 **Look at the pictures and complete the titles.**

HELP: contrasts – mausoleum[3] – flag

2 1 Track 43 **Listen and complete the captions with the information you hear.**

1. safran (épice de couleur orangée) ; 2. roue de vie (symbole des cycles de naissance, mort et réincarnation en hindouisme) ; 3. mausolée

BREAK IN VIDEO

 # vidéo
India Travel Guide
- 1'09''
foucherconnect.fr/18tten18

a. The video is about:
- ☐ India's history
- ☐ the top five destinations in India

b. The capital of India is:
- ☐ New Delhi ☐ Kerala

c. Mumbai is:
- ☐ the most cosmopolitan city in India
- ☐ "God's country"

d. The state of princes and palaces is:
- ☐ Rajasthan ☐ Agar

TÂCHE 1 **Demander ou donner des informations sur une ville indienne**

EOI – A2+

India: Past and Present

Activity A — Fast Facts

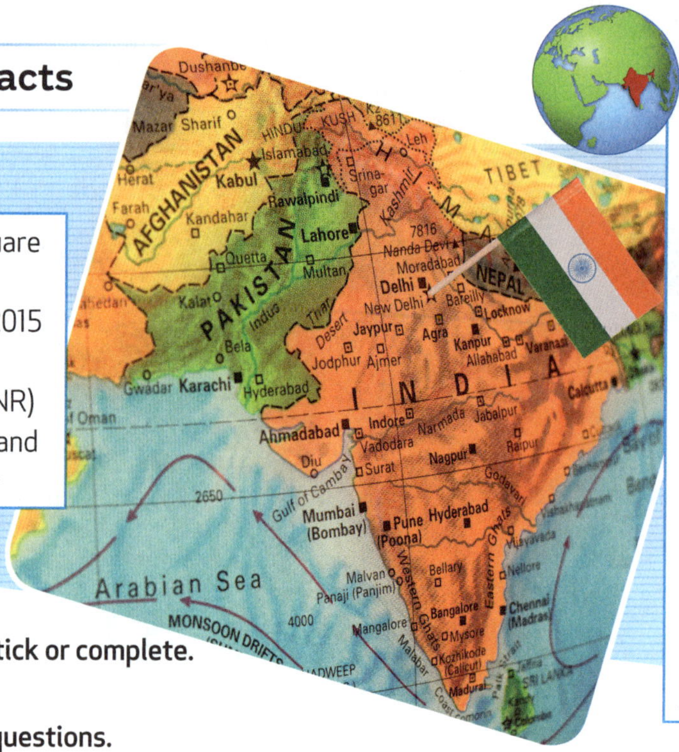

Area: 3,287,000 km² (square kilometres)
Population: 1.3 billion in 2015
1.6 billion by 2030
Currency: Indian rupee (INR)
National games: Hockey and cricket

Capital city:
☐ Chennai ☐ New Delhi
Megacities: ☐ Mumbai (formerly Bombay)
☐ Pune ☐ Agra
☐ Kolkata (formerly Calcutta)
Official languages:
Hindi, ...
Form of government:
Parliamentary ....
Religions: ....% Hindu
.......% Muslim; 2.4%
Christian; ....% Sikh;
........% other

1 Track 44 **Listen and tick or complete.**

2 **Read and answer the questions.**

a. How many inhabitants were there in 2015? ....
b. Do Indian people pay in dollars? ....
c. How big is India? ....

Activity B — Indian Traditions

....

....

....

3 Track 45 **Listen and fill in the missing information.**

a. *Namaste* is pressing your .... together with a smile in greeting. It is used as a respectful form of greeting and .... It is also used to .... people.
b. In India, cows are considered sacred and many Hindus do not eat .... Most Hindus respect cows for their .... nature and because they are very .... animals. Sacred cows can go anywhere they like: even in the .... and ....
c. Holi festival is celebrated for two or three days .... People pour coloured .... on each other and .... many types of delicious and colourful food.

4 **Use the information above to give a title to each picture.**

Activity C Timeline

1. The Moguls developed the arts and the trade of spices, rice, silk, tea and jewels.

3. Mahatma Gandhi began his campaign of non-violence against the British government.

5. Indira Gandhi became Prime Minister. She was one of the first women ever elected to lead a nation.

1526	....	....	....	1966	....

2. The British Empire took control of India.

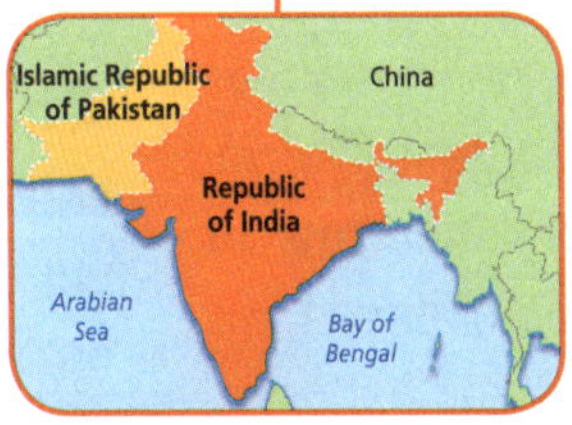

4. India became an independent nation divided into two countries: the Republic of India and the Islamic Republic of Pakistan.

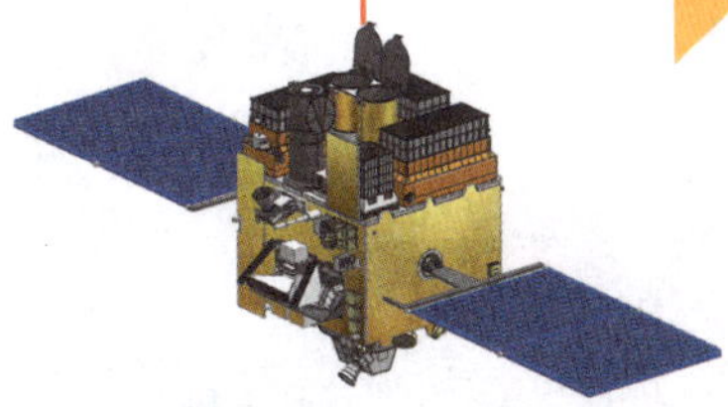

6. India launched its first space laboratory, Astrosat.

5 Track 46 Listen and fill in the missing dates in the timeline.

6 Find in the timeline the English for:

a. *Moghols* (1) : ....
b. *commerce* (1) : ....
c. *épices* (1) : ....
d. *contre* (3) : ....
e. *diriger* (5) : ....
f. *lancer* (6) : ....

7 Look at the timeline and answer the questions.

a. What sort of trade did the Moguls develop?

....

....

b. When did India become independent?

....

c. What did India launch in 2016?

....

8 Track 47 Listen and orally answer other questions about the timeline.

FOCUS

a. Indira Gandhi became Prime Minister in 1966.

b. India launched Astrosat in 2016.

- *Les verbes soulignés sont :*
  ☐ *au présent* ☐ *au prétérit*
- *Donnez leur base verbale :*

....

- *Le prétérit exprime une action :*
  ☐ *en train de se dérouler*
  ☐ *passée, datée, terminée*

c. When **did** India **become** independent?

- *À la forme interrogative, on utilise :*
  .... + *sujet* + *base verbale* + ... ?

Training ex. 3, 4, 5

NOW ACT

9 **Work in pairs.** Ask and answer questions about Mumbai and Kolkata to fill in the form.

Student A	**Student B**
Step 1 Go to **page 131**. Ask **Student B** questions to fill in the information about Mumbai.	**Step 1** Go to **page 132**. Answer **Student A**'s questions about Mumbai.
Step 2 Then answer **Student B**'s questions about Kolkata.	**Step 2** Then ask **Student A** questions to fill in the information about Kolkata.

Bollywood

Activity D Mumbai's World-Famous Movies

1. Bollywood, a contraction of 'Bombay' and 'Hollywood', is the largest film industry in terms of the number of films made and exported worldwide. In 2015, over 4 billion tickets were sold across the globe, which is almost twice as many as Hollywood.

2. Bollywood films are often longer than those made in Hollywood. The plots are usually more melodramatic. Anything can happen, so long as there's a happy ending and lots of singing and dancing.

3. In India, cinema is an integral part of the lives of millions of fans, who identify with the actors and the values they represent. The big hits are a reflection of Indian culture and morals.

4. Bollywood's unique style is becoming more and more popular all over the world. Big-budget films are now produced, like *Baahubali: The Beginning* and its sequel *Baahubali 2: The Conclusion*, which is the story of two brothers fighting for the supremacy of a medieval kingdom. This epic fantasy is high on drama, costumes, and special effects. The film opened on 9,000 screens worldwide in 2017.

1 **Answer the questions.**

a. What is the document about? ....

b. Where are Bollywood films made? ....

c. Are these films successful only in India? ....

2 **Find in the document the English for:**

a. *deux fois plus que (§1):* ....

b. *intrigue (du film) (§2):* ....

c. *de gros succès (§3):* ....

d. *des films à gros budgets (§4):* ....

3 **Tick "True" or "False".**

	True	False
a. The Bollywood film industry makes more films than Hollywood.	☐	☐
b. Bollywood sells more film tickets in the world than Hollywood.	☐	☐
c. Bollywood films are shorter than Hollywood films.	☐	☐
d. There is no singing and dancing in Bollywood films.	☐	☐

NOW ACT

4 **Go to page 133. Read the document and explain in French the characteristics of Bollywood movies.**

FOCUS

a. Bollywood films are often longer than those made in Hollywood.
b. The plots are usually more melodramatic.

- *Les adjectifs sont au :* ☐ *comparatif de supériorité = plus (que ...)*
  ☐ *superlatif de supériorité = le plus (de tous)*
- *Soulignez la terminaison de l'adjectif court.*
- *L'adjectif long est précédé de* ....

Training ex. 6, 7

TÂCHE 3 Comprendre un reportage sur une start-up de Mumbai

CO – A2+

VIDEO TIME 5

A Startup in Mumbai

 # vidéo
Startup Gives Mumbai Taxis a Makeover – 2'26''
foucherconnect.fr/18tten19

Step 1 Before watching the video.

1 Look at the picture above and read the title of the video. Then make hypotheses about the topic of the video in English or in French.

....

....

....

....

Step 2 Watch the whole video.

2 Tick "True" or "False".

	True	False
a. There is a lot of traffic in Mumbai.	☐	☐
b. The insides of these taxis look pretty much the same.	☐	☐
c. The startup is not very successful.	☐	☐
d. The young entrepreneur says he is a designer.	☐	☐
e. The startup has grand ideas for expansion.	☐	☐

Step 3 Watch the video up to 0:22.

3 Answer the questions.

a. What is the atmosphere like in Mumbai?

....

b. How many inhabitants are there in Mumbai?

....

c. How many of them take taxis every day?

....

....

Step 4 Watch the video from 0:22 to 0:44.

4 Circle the correct words.

(*Outside* / *Inside*), these taxis all look pretty much the same.

Go (*outside* / *inside*) and you'll discover some have had a drastic (*renovation* / *makeover*).

Reporter: - Now, I'm starting to see that the (*canvas* / *fabric*) is everywhere.

Entrepreneur: - Yes, it's all about what's put you into this (*cocoon* / *decoration*) when you enter, you know.

HELP!

an auto rickshaw un pousse-pousse motorisé
a cab un taxi
canvas de la toile (tissu)
a cocoon un cocon
a commute un trajet maison-travail
drastic drastique, radical
fabric du tissu
festoon décorer, orner
a makeover un relooking
a tuk-tuk un pousse-pousse

Fiche VIDEO TIME 5 *A Startup in Mumbai* complète disponible en téléchargement

UNIT 5 Training

exo
foucherconnect.fr/18tten20

IN TUNE

A 1 Track 48 Écoutez la prononciation des mots interrogatifs "how" /h/ et "what" /w/. Puis répétez.

B 1 Track 49 Écoutez et classez les mots interrogatifs en fonction de leur prononciation. Puis répétez.

	which	who	where	when	whose	why
/w/						
/h/						

1 Associez la question à la rubrique correspondante.

a. Is it a republic or a kingdom? ○
b. How many inhabitants are there? ○
c. How big is the country? ○
d. Do they speak English? ○
e. Do they pay in Euros? ○

○ **1.** Area
○ **2.** Currency
○ **3.** Form of government
○ **4.** Population
○ **5.** Language

2 Complétez cette grille à l'aide des illustrations.

5

6

1

2

3

4

7

8

3 Indiquez si les verbes sont réguliers (R) ou irréguliers (IR) et écrivez leur prétérit.

a. discover (....): ....
b. tell (....): ....
c. look (....): ....
d. start (....): ....
e. know (....): ....
f. take (....): ....
g. work (....): ....

Vocabulary

Nouns
area la superficie
currency la devise, la monnaie du pays
faith la foi
a flag un drapeau
a greeting un salut
an issue un problème, un enjeu
a megacity une très grande ville, une métropole
trade le commerce

Verbs
become* devenir
be* divided into être divisé en
begin*/start commencer
date back to remonter à
lead* mener, diriger
take* control of prendre le contrôle, la direction de

Adjectives
lively animé, gai, vivant
noisy bruyant

Adverbs
formerly anciennement
yet cependant

Others
dozens of des douzaines de
tens of des centaines de
thousands of des milliers de
twice deux fois

4 **Complétez en conjuguant les verbes au prétérit.**

a. Before 1972, Sri Lanka's name .... Ceylon. (*be*)

b. In the 18th century, the British .... coffee and tea plantations. (*develop*)

c. The country .... independent in 1948. (*become*)

d. In 1965, the country .... 200,000 tonnes of tea. (*export*)

e. In 2009, after a long civil war, the country .... to expand again. (*begin*)

5 **Complétez les questions portant sur les éléments soulignés.**

a. New Delhi became the capital city of India <u>in 1931</u>.
When ....
....

b. New Delhi hosted <u>the Cricket World Cup</u> in 2011.
What ....

c. A legend says that King Dhilu <u>built the city</u> and named it after himself.
What ....

6 1 Track 50 **Écoutez et complétez les informations manquantes.**

	Canada	USA
Population	.... million	325 million
Area	.... million km²	9.83 million km²
Highest mountain	Mount Logan .... m	Mount McKinley 6,190 m
Tallest building	CN Tower .... m	One World Trade Center 546 m

7 **Complétez les phrases pour comparer le Canada et les USA. Mettez les adjectifs au comparatif et utilisez les informations du tableau (ex. 6).**

a. (populous): USA is ....
....

b. (big): Canada is ....
....

c. (high): Mount McKinley is ....
....

d. (tall): The CN Tower is ....
....

Language TIPS

Le prétérit

→ **exprimer une action ou un état daté, passé, terminé**

- **avec *be* :** **Were you in India in 2010? No, I wasn't. I was in China.** *Étiez-vous en Inde en 2010 ? Non, j'étais en Chine.*

- **avec un verbe régulier :** **Why did Gandhi campaign in 1915? He campaign<u>ed</u> because he want<u>ed</u> India to be independent.** *Pourquoi Gandhi a-t-il fait campagne en 1915 ? Il a fait campagne car il voulait que l'inde soit indépendante.*

- **avec un verbe irrégulier* :** **Did Bollywood begin in 1945? No, it didn't. It began in 1913.** *Est-ce que Bollywood a commencé en 1945 ? Non, cela a commencé en 1913.*

Le comparatif de supériorité : plus... (que)

→ **Adjectif court : adj. *-er* (+ *than*)**

Series are short<u>er</u> and often funn<u>ier</u> than films. *Les séries sont plus courtes et souvent plus drôles que les films.*

→ **Adjectif long : *more* + adj. (+ *than*)**

Costumes are <u>more</u> amazing in Bollywood movies than in western movies. *Les costumes sont plus étonnants dans les films de Bollywood que dans les films occidentaux.*

→ ***good* ▶ *better* / *bad* ▶ *worse***

Now, he is better at swimming than his friend. But he is worse at running. *Il est désormais meilleur à la nage que son ami. Mais il est pire à la course.*

* *Voir liste des verbes irréguliers sur les rabats*

FINAL TASK 5 Play Jeopardy

SCENARIO Dans le cadre de la semaine des langues, vous devez réaliser un jeu de *Jeopardy* sur le thème des pays étrangers.

RÈGLES DU JEU
À partir de réponses (indices), les joueurs doivent trouver la question correspondante. Chaque bonne question rapporte des points, mais chaque erreur en fait perdre. Les joueurs peuvent choisir une catégorie et un nombre de points.

Étape 1 Trouver des informations sur un pays CE – A2+

- Choisissez un pays que vous connaissez ou qui vous attire.
- Recherchez sur Internet les informations utiles pour compléter la fiche ci-dessous.

Country:	
Geography	• Location: .... • Capital city and megacities: .... • Population: .... • Area: ....
Famous for:	• Traditions: .... • Culture (literature, cinema, music, dance…): .... • Sports: .... • Monuments: .... • Personalities: ....
Important events	Events: .... / .... / .... / .... Dates: .... / .... / .... / ....

Étape 2 Réaliser un jeu de *Jeopardy* EE – A2+

Pour réaliser votre jeu, utilisez les documents disponibles en téléchargement.

- Sélectionnez trois indices par rubrique (*Geography / Famous for / Important Events*) et attribuez-leur des points : 100, 300 ou 500.
- Préparez les cartes. Inscrivez au dos de chaque carte l'indice que le joueur pourra lire.
- Écrivez sur un autre document les questions que le joueur devra poser pour obtenir les points correspondant aux indices.

Étape 3 Jouer au *Jeopardy* EOI – A2+

- Vous serez le meneur de jeu pour le *Jeopardy* que vous avez réalisé. Chaque joueur choisira sa carte et vous vérifierez la question posée. Vous attribuerez les points convenus si la question est correcte ou retirerez les points s'il y a une erreur.
- À votre tour, vous jouerez également sur les jeux réalisés par les autres élèves.

mon bilan UNIT 5

	J'ai réussi à…	−−	−	+	++
EOI	Demander ou donner des informations sur une ville				
CE	Comprendre des informations sur le cinéma en Inde				
CO	Comprendre un reportage sur une start-up de Mumbai				
EE	Réaliser un jeu de *Jeopardy*				

UNIT 5

S'exprimer sur un pays à partir de mots-clés

CCF PREP 9

PARTIE 1 EOC

LET'S TRAIN!

1. ....

New Zealand is a wealthy[1] nation dominated by.................... cultural groups: New Zealanders, the descendants of.............................. people; and the Maori, the descendants of Polynesian people.

2. ....

It is situated in the.......................... Pacific ocean.

3. ....

The country is made up of........... large islands and smaller ones. The...................... city is ....

4. ....

.... is the main source of income[2], but manufacturing and...................... are developing.

5. ....

Because of the islands' geographical isolation, many of the plants and .... are unique to the country, like the kiwi which is the......................... of the nation.

6. ....

The British Empire took control of New Zealand in 1840. The country became independent in 1947.

7. ....

Queen Elizabeth II is still officially the head of state, but she is represented by a governor-general. New Zealand is a .... democracy and Jacinda Ardern is the..............................

1. *riche* ; 2. *principale source de revenus*

1 1 Track 51 **Écoutez et complétez les informations sur la Nouvelle-Zélande.**

2 **Ajoutez le titre de chaque paragraphe.**

HELP!: Location – Economy – People's origins – Independence – Geography – Government – Nature

3 **Soulignez les mots-clés (informations essentielles) du document.**

4 **Notez les mots-clés que vous avez soulignés sur une feuille de brouillon. Puis, entraînez-vous à parler de la Nouvelle-Zélande à partir de ces mots.**

YOUR TURN!

5 **Utilisez les mots-clés donnés pour présenter l'île de Malte.**

Malta

• **Location**	>>>>>>>>>	Mediterranean Sea / south of the island of Sicily
• **Geography**	>>>>>>>	Two large islands
• **Capital city**	>>>>>>>	Valletta
• **Economy**	>>>>>>>>>	Tourism
• **British Empire**	>>>>>	1814
• **Independence**	>>>>>	1964

CCF PREP 10

PARTIE 2 EOI

Répondre à des questions sur un pays

LET'S TRAIN!

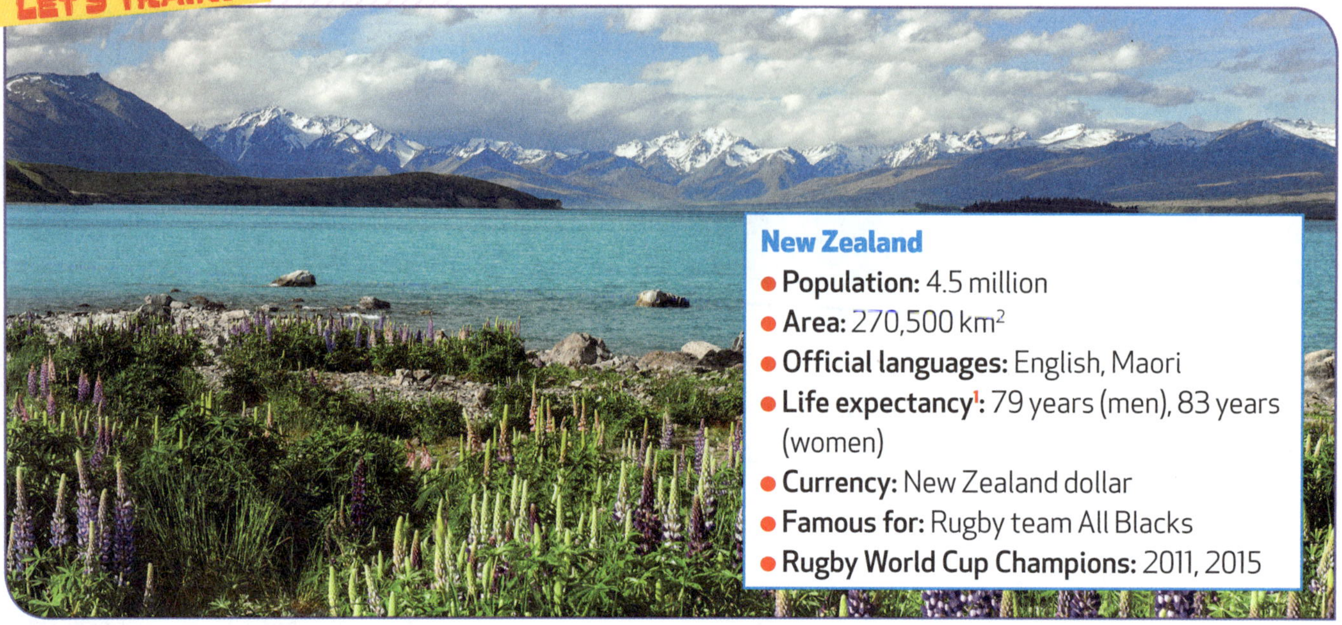

New Zealand
- **Population:** 4.5 million
- **Area:** 270,500 km^2
- **Official languages:** English, Maori
- **Life expectancy**[1]**:** 79 years (men), 83 years (women)
- **Currency:** New Zealand dollar
- **Famous for:** Rugby team All Blacks
- **Rugby World Cup Champions:** 2011, 2015

1. *espérance de vie*

1 Track 52 Répondez aux questions enregistrées.

a. ……………………………………………………………………………

b. ……………………………………………………………………………

c. ……………………………………………………………………………

d. ……………………………………………………………………………

e. ……………………………………………………………………………

2 Travaillez par deux et utilisez les éléments donnés pour poser d'autres questions à l'oral.

YOUR TURN!

3 Lisez le document sur Malte et préparez cinq questions à poser à votre partenaire. Puis posez-lui vos questions et répondez aux siennes.

Malta
- **Population:** 419,000
- **Area:** 316 km^2
- **Main languages:** Maltese, English
- **Currency:** Euro
- **Life expectancy:** 78 years (men), 82 years (women)
- **Government:** unitary parliamentary republic
- **President:** Marie-Louise Coleiro Preca
- **Member of the European Union:** 2004
- **Famous for:** its many historical monuments

Your questions:

1. ……………………………………………
2. ……………………………………………
3. ……………………………………………
4. ……………………………………………
5. ……………………………………………

UNIT 6

TÂCHE FINALE Présenter une ville intelligente à l'aide d'un diaporama

EOC – A2+

Smart Cities

ENGLAND

City: ....

DENMARK

City: ....

CHINA

City: ....

1 **Fill in the labels with the names of the cities.**

Copenhagen *Hong Kong* *Bristol*

2 2 Track 1 **Listen and match the three key aspects of a smart city with their definitions.**

Smart grid	○	○	a city with varied, efficient and environmentally friendly public transport.
Connected city	○	○	an environmentally friendly city with well-developed recycling bins and aiming for a low carbon impact, for instance.
Green city	○	○	a city with easy access to the internet to check transport apps, for example.

3 2 Track 2 **Listen and fill in the labels on the pictures with the characteristics of each city.**

smart grid *green city* *connected city*

BREAK IN VIDEO

 # vidéo
Smart Cities: Step into the City of the Future – 2'00''
foucherconnect.fr/18tten21

a. **The video is about:**
☐ common cities ☐ smart cities

b. **One issue for smart cities is:**
☐ pollution ☐ agriculture

c. **A smart city is:**
☐ hyper-connected ☐ old

d. **The main goal of smart cities is to improve the lives of their:** ☐ citizens ☐ animals

Smart Innovations

Activity A Great Apps!

(a) .... app

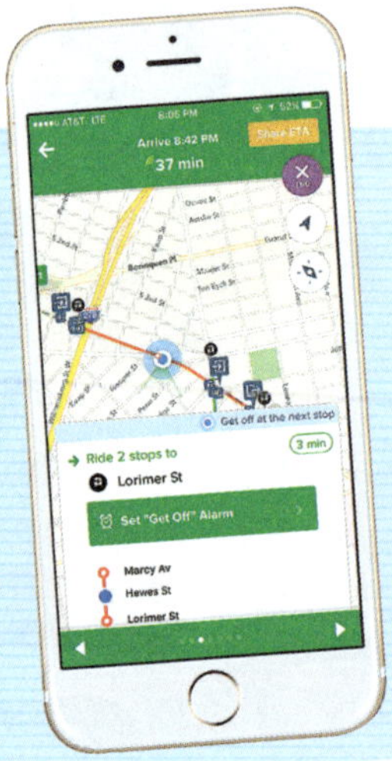

(b) .... app

(c) .... app

1 **Look at the apps and complete the stickers with:**

Transport *Weather* *Going out*

2 2 Track 3 **Write the letters corresponding to the definitions of the apps.**

a. This app helps you to commute[1]. It gives bus timetables, for example. (.....)

b. This app helps you to check the temperature outside for instance. (.....)

c. This app helps you to book tickets for shows. (.....)

1. *Effectuer un aller-retour pour aller au travail*

Activity B Smart Transport in Barcelona

3 2 Track 4 **Listen and tick the right answers.**

a. Bicing is:

☐ a bicycle-renting[1] system

☐ a car-renting system

b. The city has developed the number of:

☐ electric cars ☐ bus routes

c. The system works:

☐ with small CCTV cameras

☐ with sensors[2] in the pavements[3]

d. The last app is used to check:

☐ traffic ☐ speed limits

1. *location* ; 2. *capteur* ; 3. *trottoir*

Activity C — Welcome to One of the Greenest Cities Ever!

GREENHOUSE GAS RATE

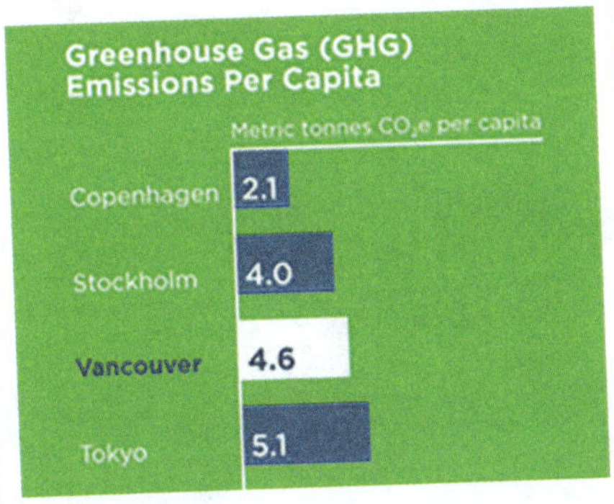

.... rate in the world.

GEOGRAPHICAL SITUATION

Country: ....

City: ....

Number of inhabitants: more than ....

PROGRAMME

ZEROWASTE

- develop .... collection;
- upgrade .... bins.

GOAL

50% of trips on foot, by bicycle or on ....

ENERGY

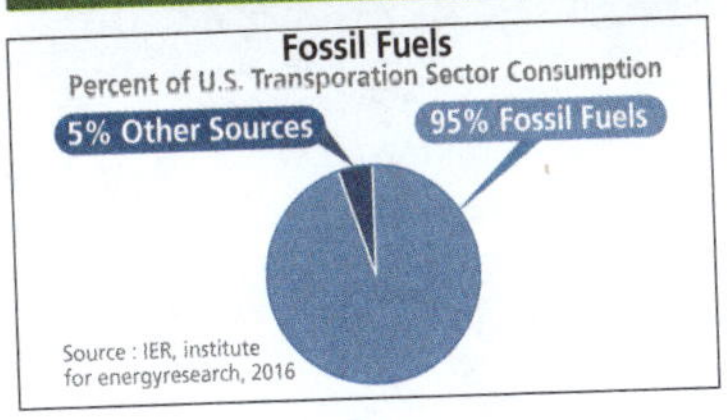

.... rate in the world.

4 2 Track 5 **Listen and number the slides in the order they are presented.**

5 2 Track 5 **Listen again and complete the slides with the information you hear.**

6 2 Track 5 **Listen again and complete the sentences below to introduce each slide.**

a. ...., we can see on the first slide...

b. On the second ...., we can see...

c. .... on the third...

d. The fourth slide ....

e. .... is a slide about...

NOW ACT

7 **Use the elements from the exercises above to present the city of Vancouver.**

FOCUS

a. Vancouver has the lowest greenhouse effect rate.

b. It is the most eco-friendly city in North America.

- *Le superlatif se forme de la façon suivante :*
  - .... + *adjectif court* + - .... : **a**
  - .... + *adjectif long* : **b**

Training ex. 5, 6

The Evolution of a Smart City

Activity D San Francisco

MORE DEVELOPMENTS AHEAD

The city must improve its transport system

San Francisco has faced many issues in terms of smart transport over the years. In February 2017, the city was even dubbed[1] the fourth most-congested city in the world according to The Washington-based traffic data company INRIX. Moreover, other statistics show that vehicles are parked 95% of the time, which raises another problem of parking spaces.

To try to solve—or at least reduce—these problems, the city must hurry and has put into place a series of programs.

For example, people can download a smart app called "MUNI[2] mobile". With this app, they can pay for their tickets and plan the quickest itinerary but they can't rent a bike. To do that, people can go to Fordgobike.com or download the app and check availability, prices, etc.

In addition, the city is also thinking ahead and is working with students, who are developing a car-sharing app. This app will link people so they can share a trip in the same car. A step further in managing traffic congestion.

1. surnommé ; 2. San Francisco Municipal Railway

1 Tick the right answer.

This article is about:

☐ housing in San Francisco
☐ transport in San Francisco

2 Find in the document the English for:

a. *(§1) problèmes:* ....
b. *(§2) régler/résoudre:* ....
c. *(§3) vérifier:* ....
d. *(§4) faire le lien:* ....
e. *(§4) partager:* ....
f. *(§4) embouteillage:* ....

3 Read the first paragraph and answer the questions.

a. What are the transport problems in San Francisco?

....

....

b. What was San Francisco dubbed?

....

....

c. What does 95% represent?

....

....

4 Underline in the text:

a. what the city has done to help with problems.
b. what people can do with MUNI mobile.
c. what people can do with Fordgobike.com.

FOCUS

a. San Francisco must hurry.
b. They can't rent a bike.
c. They can pay for their tickets.

- *L'énoncé* **a** *exprime une :* ☐ *obligation* ☐ *possibilité* ☐ *impossibilité*
  L'énoncé **b** *exprime une :* ☐ *obligation* ☐ *possibilité* ☐ *impossibilité*
  L'énoncé **c** *exprime une :* ☐ *obligation* ☐ *possibilité* ☐ *impossibilité*
- *Les mots soulignés sont des :* ☐ *verbes* ☐ *modaux*

Training ex. 3, 4

NOW ACT

5 Read the summary on page 133 and correct the wrong information.

TÂCHE 3 **Comprendre une vidéo sur le palmarès des villes intelligentes**

CO – B1

VIDEO TIME 6

The Most Eco-friendly Cities

 # vidéo
10 Smartest Cities In The World – 2'02''
foucherconnect.fr/18tten22

Step 1 **Before watching the video.**

1 Read the title of the video and make hypotheses about the topic.

....

....

....

....

....

....

....

....

Step 2 **Watch the whole video.**

2 Underline the correct answers.

a. The video is about the (*five* / *ten*) smartest cities in (*the world* / *in the USA*).

b. The three smartest cities are (*London* / *Vienna* / *Copenhagen* / *Paris* / *Toronto*).

c. The cities are ranked by a website called (*livingtogether.com* /*co-exist.com*).

Step 3 **Watch the video up to 0:22.**

3 Choose the right answers.

a. Barcelona is a:
☐ pioneer ☐ beginner as a smart city

b. In Hong Kong, people can pay with a smart:
☐ pass ☐ card

Step 4 **Watch the video from 0:22 to 0:43.**

4 Complete the script.

a. Number .... is Copenhagen.

b. The city has committed to carbon neutrality by ....

c. .... of its citizens regularly commute by bicycle.

d. Berlin is ....

HELP!

carbon neutrality la neutralité carbone
a pioneer un(e) pionnier(ère)
a power plant une centrale électrique
quality la qualité
a ranking un classement
sustainability la durabilité

Fiche VIDEO TIME 6 *The Most Eco-friendly Cities* complète disponible en téléchargement

UNIT 6

Training

\# exo
foucherconnect.fr/18tten23

IN TUNE

A 2 Track 6 **Écoutez et répétez.**

can /kæn/ can't /ka:nt/ must /mʌst/ mustn't /mʌsnt/

B 2 Track 7 **Écoutez et cochez les modaux utilisés.**

	Can /kæn/	Can't /ka:nt/	Must /mʌst/	Mustn't /mʌsnt/
a.				
b.				
c.				
d.				

C 2 Track 8 **Écoutez et répétez les phrases.**

1 **Associez chaque expression à son (ses) domaine(s) (a, b, c).**

a. **Smart grid** b. **Connected city** c. **Green city**

Carbon emissions: ☐ a ☐ b ☐ c
WIFi connection: ☐ a ☐ b ☐ c
Large choice of transport: ☐ a ☐ b ☐ c
Smart parking spots: ☐ a ☐ b ☐ c
Traffic apps: ☐ a ☐ b ☐ c
Development of recycling bins: ☐ a ☐ b ☐ c

2 **Complétez les phrases avec les éléments donnés en légende des photos.**

a. The city has developed its .... which is good for the environment.
b. To avoid parking problems, ... is convenient.
c. I hate being stuck in ....
d. I have a new telephone; I am going to download plenty of new ....

Apps

Recycling bins

Renting electrical car

Traffic congestion

Vocabulary

Nouns
an app une appli
an appliance un appareil
CO_2 emissions émissions de dioxyde de carbone
a device un appareil, un dispositif
litter des détritus
a parking spot une place de parking
a pavement un trottoir
a recycling bin une poubelle pour le recyclage
a safety issue un problème de sécurité
a sensor un capteur
traffic congestion un/des embouteillage(s)
waste les ordures

Verbs
check vérifier
recycle recycler
reduce réduire
rent louer
upgrade mettre à jour

Adjectives
polluting polluant
smart intelligent

3 Soulignez le modal qui convient.

a. In Barcelona, you (can't / can) rent a bike.
b. A smart city (must / can't) reduce its CO_2 emissions.
c. To reduce pollution, people (mustn't / can) use plastic bags.
d. To avoid traffic congestion, drivers (can / can't) check an app.
e. People (must / can't) use a recycling bin in cities.

4 Complétez avec le modal *must* ou *can*.

a. A smart city .... be connected.
b. Inhabitants in Hong Kong .... check a traffic app.
c. People .... recycle in smart cities.
d. CCTV .... be an issue in smart cities.

5 Entourez la bonne réponse.

a. **green:** adjectif court / adjectif long
b. **eco-friendly:** adjectif court / adjectif long
c. **intelligent:** adjectif court / adjectif long
d. **easy:** adjectif court / adjectif long
e. **smart:** adjectif court / adjectif long
f. **efficient:** adjectif court / adjectif long

6 Complétez les phrases en mettant l'adjectif entre parenthèses au superlatif.

a. Hong Kong is one of .... cities. (smart)
b. Transport must be .... (eco-friendly)
c. This app is .... to use. (easy)
d. Hydropower is .... energy. (green)

7 Find the words corresponding to the definitions.

a. Object in which you recycle waste: ....
b. It helps you check the weather on your telephone: ....
c. The internet network in a smart city: ....
d. When you are stuck in transport: ....

Language TIPS

Le superlatif

→ The + *adjectif court* + -est
It is the smartest city in Europe.
C'est la ville la plus intelligente d'Europe.
It is the busiest area in the town.
C'est l'endroit le plus peuplé de la ville.

→ The most + *adjectif long*
It is the most amazing city in America.
C'est la ville la plus fantastique d'Amérique.

→ The best / the worst
It is the best app ever!
C'est la meilleure des applications !
It is the worst connected city!
C'est la pire ville connectée !

Les modaux

→ Exprimer une obligation
You must recycle paper.
Tu dois recycler le papier.

→ Exprimer une possibilité
You can use an electrical car.
Tu peux utiliser une voiture électrique.

→ Exprimer une interdiction
You can't / mustn't use the internet.
Tu ne peux pas / ne dois pas utiliser Internet.

FINAL TASK 6

Present a Smart City

SCENARIO À l'occasion d'une exposition sur les villes intelligentes organisée au sein de votre établissement, vous devez présenter la ville intelligente de votre choix.

Étape 1 Compléter une fiche EE – A2+

- Cherchez des informations sur une ville intelligente de votre choix et complétez la fiche ci-dessous pour préparer votre diaporama.

SLIDE 1 General information	SLIDE 2 Green numbers
Name: .... Country: .... Geographical situation: .... Number of inhabitants:	Current greenhouse gas rate: .... Other numbers regarding current energy consumption: ....
SLIDE 3 Smart grid/Public transport	**SLIDE 4 Daily life environmental measures**
Innovation in terms of transport and traffic congestion: ☐ car rental ☐ parking spots ☐ development of bus routes ☐ other:	Development of waste recycling bins, measures around water consumption, etc.: ....
SLIDE 5 Energy	
Type of sources used to produce electricity (water, wind, etc.):	

Étape 2 Réaliser un diaporama EE – A2+

- Illustrez chaque diapositive avec des photos, des dessins, des schémas, des graphiques, etc.
- Ne rédigez pas de phrases complètes. Vous pouvez noter quelques informations essentielles (titres, chiffres, etc.).

Étape 3 Présenter une ville intelligente à partir de votre diaporama EOC – A2+

- Entraînez-vous à présenter votre diaporama. Utilisez les informations de chaque diapositive pour expliquer les particularités de la ville choisie. Soignez votre prononciation et votre intonation.
- Présentez votre diaporama en vous enregistrant avec votre téléphone ou un lecteur MP3.

mon bilan UNIT 6

	J'ai réussi à…	−−	−	+	++
EOC	Présenter les différents éléments d'une ville intelligente				
CE	Comprendre un article sur le développement d'une ville intelligente				
CO	Comprendre une vidéo sur le palmarès des villes intelligentes				

UNIT 6

S'exprimer à partir d'un diaporama

CCF PREP 11

PARTIE 1 EOC

LET'S TRAIN!

"The .... of my presentation is the city of Vienna."

1. Geographical Situation

.................................., there is a map of Vienna, in Austria.

2. Headquarters

The UN has one of its four headquarters there, ...
....

3. Transport

.................................., Vienna has 850 kilometres of public transport.

4. Communication

Free Wi-Fi ....
....
....

5. Upcoming Project 1

LED lamps in every street.

6. Upcoming Project 2

Electric taxi fleets

7. Conclusion

Won Most Admired Knowledge City in 2015.

8. Acknowledgement

1 2 Track 9 **Écoutez la présentation et complétez l'introduction et les diapositives 1 à 4.**

2 2 Track 10 **Écoutez et répétez la présentation des diapositives 5 à 8.**

YOUR TURN!

3 **Utilisez les éléments des diapositives suivantes pour faire une présentation orale.**

Copenhagen

Public transport: large offer, reliable

Wi-Fi is available almost everywhere

Energy: 10% of the nation's electricity is produced by offshore wind turbines*

* éoliennes en mer

CCF PREP 12

PARTIE 3 CE

Comprendre un article sur les villes intelligentes en Inde

Pros and Cons of a Plan about Indian Smart Cities

Pros

The usage of technology would allow a city to run itself efficiently and provide a partial solution to the various problems plaguing[1] our cities. These include traffic, pollution, water supply, electricity supply, industrialization, etc. [...]

A smart city would theoretically use CCTV cameras, hotlines, panic buttons and identification systems to ensure the security of its population. [...] A smart city would be able to keep criminals out using CCTV.

Cons

Corruption might just become more sophisticated and lead to all the benefits being washed away[2]. [...]

There are a huge number of cities in India that could theoretically be the smart cities we think of. Upgrading cities like Mumbai and Delhi [...] would be far more beneficial than creating new ones. Extremely high-rise apartment blocks should be encouraged to conserve land around these places. India is a small country and can't afford to lose more agricultural or forest land.

There is a risk that the gap between the poor and the rich might increase[3], especially if the working classes can't find any place in the new cities.

https://declara.com, November 12, 2017.

1. *ronger* ; **2.** *enlever* ; **3.** *augmenter*

Répondez aux questions en français.

1. De quoi parle le texte ?

....

....

2. Quels seraient les avantages de l'utilisation des nouvelles technologies ?

....

....

3. Quels sont les avantages des caméras de surveillance ?

....

....

4. Quels seraient les inconvénients pour l'Inde de développer des villes intelligentes ?

....

....

....

5. Quelle est, pour l'auteur, la chose à faire plutôt que de construire des villes nouvelles ?

....

6. Quel problème pourront rencontrer les classes moyennes ?

....

South Africa, the Rainbow Nation

Culture CLICK 3

The term "Rainbow Nation" is used to describe the new .... in South Africa. It is represented by the South African .... which shows .... different colours and symbolizes people coming from different cultures and .... that go together in the same ....

1 **Look at the flag and use the words below to fill in the document.**
HELP! six – unity – direction – flag – horizons

1. Table Mountain
a flat-top mountain overlooking ....
....

3. Soweto
South Western
....
of Johannesburg

2. Cradle of Humankind
famous archeological .... in the north-west of Johannesburg

4. Kruger National Park
located in the north-east of the country, it is the largest game .... in Africa

2 2 Track 11 **Listen and fill in the missing words. Then write the corresponding numbers in the map labels below.**

Official name: ....
Administrative Capital: ....
Largest City: ....
Official languages: .... (including Zulu, Afrikaans, Xhosa and ....)
Number of inhabitants: about ....
Ethnic groups: ....% Black, ...%..... Coloured, ...% White, ...% Asian
End of apartheid*: ....
Currency: Rand

* *racial segregation separating white people from black and coloured people (different jobs, houses, schools...).*

3 2 Track 12 **Listen and fill in the missing information about South Africa.**

Quiz

1 **South Africa shares a border with:**
a. 5 countries ☐
b. 6 countries ☐
c. 7 countries ☐

2 **Of all the countries in Africa, South Africa is:**
a. the most diverse ☐
b. the poorest ☐
c. the wealthiest ☐

3 **The language most spoken is:**
a. Zulu ☐
b. English ☐
c. Afrikaans ☐

4 **In the 16th century, the first Europeans settled near:**
a. Cape Town ☐
b. Port Elizabeth ☐
c. Durban ☐

5 **King Protea, the national flower, can have a diameter up to:**
a. 20 cm ☐
b. 30 cm ☐
c. 50 cm ☐

6 **The country is famous for its mines of:**
a. gold and diamonds ☐
b. silver and diamonds ☐
c. diamonds and uranium ☐

7 **Park Kruger National Park covers an area of:**
a. 5,900 km² ☐
b. 12,700 km² ☐
c. 19,500 km² ☐

8 **In South Africa, you can find:**
a. zebras, giraffes and tigers ☐
b. lions, elephants and rhinos ☐
c. rhinos, hippos and koalas ☐

9 **In 1967 in Cape Town, Professor Barnard performed the first human:**
a. hand transplant ☐
b. heart transplant ☐
c. eye transplant ☐

10 **The most popular sport in South Africa is:**
a. soccer ☐
b. rugby ☐
c. cricket ☐

2 Track 14 **Listen and check.**

Your score: … /10

Mandela: Father of the Nation

Nelson Mandela was the son of a tribal chief. His father died when he was nine. Nelson went to college and studied law.

Mandela soon began to protest against the apartheid established by the white men who governed South Africa in 1948. After several years of political action, he was arrested in 1963 and sentenced to life in prison.

Mandela refused to give up his hope and dreams for a free South Africa. Various organizations in the world protested against the white rule and supported Mandela's fight for democracy and equality.

Mandela was finally released in 1990 and apartheid was abolished in 1991. In 1993 Mandela and President FW de Klerk jointly won the Nobel Peace Prize. In 1994, Mandela was elected President after the first democratic elections in South Africa. He served as President from 1994 to 1999. His government promulgated a new constitution and worked for reconciliation between the country's racial groups. He died in 2013 at the age of 95.

4 **Read the text and answer the questions.**

a. Why was Mandela imprisoned?

……………………………………………………

b. How long did he stay in prison?

……………………………………………………

c. In your opinion, why is he called the father of the nation?

……………………………………………………

……………………………………………………

……………………………………………………

……………………………………………………

5 2 Track 13 **Listen and tick "True" or "False".**

	True	False
a. The South African soccer team is nicknamed the Springboks.	☐	☐
b. Springboks are gazelles that can jump up to two metres in the air.	☐	☐
c. The South African team was blacklisted for a long time because of the policy of apartheid.	☐	☐
d. The team was champion in 1995 for their second participation in the World Cup.	☐	☐
e. The team won the World Cup again in France in 2007.	☐	☐

Comment s'exprimer spontanément à l'oral

FICHE **AP 3**

Méthode

1 N'ayez pas peur de faire des fautes en parlant.
Il est tout à fait normal de faire des erreurs : on ne peut pas apprendre sans faire de fautes !

2 Faites des phrases courtes.
Exprimez-vous simplement et directement.

3 N'essayez pas de traduire des phrases françaises en anglais.
Au contraire, cherchez à utiliser des mots et expressions simples que vous connaissez en anglais.

4 Soignez votre prononciation.
Articulez bien. Ne parlez pas trop vite.

5 En cas d'hésitation, utilisez des *gapfillers*. A
Il est normal d'hésiter, de chercher ses mots. Apprenez quelques expressions pour vous donner le temps de réfléchir et rendre votre parole plus naturelle.

6 Demandez à votre interlocuteur de répéter. B
Si vous n'êtes pas sûr(e) d'avoir compris, n'hésitez pas à lui poser des questions.

7 Apprenez à exprimer vos réactions. C
Réagissez avec naturel en apprenant quelques expressions pour parler de vos sentiments.

8 Donnez votre avis D
Apprenez quelques expressions pour défendre votre point de vue.

9 Lancez-vous !
Ne parlez qu'en anglais pendant quelques minutes !

Vos outils

#audio foucherconnect.fr/18tten24

A Utiliser des *gapfillers*

Err… *Euh…*
Well… *Eh bien…*
You know… *Tu comprends/vous comprenez…*
You see… *Tu vois/vous voyez…*
What I mean is that… *Ce que je veux dire c'est que…*

B Demander de répéter

Sorry. Can you repeat please? *Désolé. Peux-tu répéter, s'il te plaît ?*
Please speak up! *Parlez plus fort, s'il vous plaît !*
Sorry. I didn't understand. *Désolé, je n'ai pas compris.*

C Exprimer ses réactions

Lucky you! *Veinard !*
Poor you! *Pauvre de toi !*
How incredible! *C'est incroyable !*
Wow, that's amazing! *Waouh, c'est époustouflant !*
That's absolutely fantastic/terrible! *C'est absolument fantastique/affreux!*

D Donner son avis

I think/I believe… *Je pense/Je crois…*
In my opinion/To my mind… *À mon avis/ Pour moi*
I agree with you. *Je suis d'accord.*
You are absolutely right. *Tu as tout à fait raison.*
I don't really agree with you. *Je ne suis pas vraiment d'accord.*

● **Écoutez attentivement les expressions ci-dessus et entraînez-vous à les répéter. Puis essayez de mémoriser au moins huit expressions que vous utiliserez au verso.**

FICHE AP 3

Comment s'exprimer spontanément à l'oral

Entraînez-vous !

Chronométrez chaque conversation
2 minutes : c'est bien !
3 minutes : bravo !
5 minutes : super !

● **Choisissez un rôle et essayez de parler spontanément en utilisant les conseils et expressions donnés au recto.**

Jeu de rôle 1 What to Offer a Friend?

Rôle A : Un(e) de vos ami(e)s vous a invité(e) à son anniversaire. Vous souhaitez lui offrir un beau cadeau. Vous demandez conseil à l'élève B. Vous répondez à ses questions afin de déterminer ensemble le ou les cadeaux qui pourraient lui faire plaisir.

Rôle B : L'élève A vous demande conseil car il (elle) est invité(e) à l'anniversaire d'un(e) ami(e) et souhaite lui offrir un beau cadeau. Posez-lui des questions pour mieux connaître les goûts de son ami(e). En fonction de sa personnalité, suggérerez-lui des idées de cadeau.

HELP	
Rôle A I'm invited at a birthday party offer a nice gift Could you help me / suggest me ideas? I would like to offer … / to spend … My friend likes … I don't want to spend so much money. No, I don't think that's a good idea… I think that could be a good idea. I could buy… / ask …	**Rôle B** Who is your friend? What does he/she like? Music? Cinema? Sport? Reading? How much would you like to pay? You could offer a concert / cinema / match ticket. You could go to … (name of a shop). Maybe you could buy a gift coupon at … You could invite him/her at …

Jeu de rôle 2 How to Decorate Your Bedroom?

Rôle A : Vous allez avoir la possibilité de décorer et d'aménager votre nouvelle chambre. Vous avez des idées mais vous hésitez encore sur certains points. Vous demandez à l'élève B de vous aider dans vos choix afin d'ébaucher ensemble un projet.

Rôle B : L'élève A vous demande conseil pour décorer et aménager sa chambre. Vous lui demandez quelles sont ses couleurs préférées, comment il (elle) souhaite décorer les murs de sa chambre, comment il souhaite placer ses meubles et autres objets. Vous l'aidez à ébaucher un projet de décoration et d'aménagement.

HELP	
Rôle A decorate / install / arrange my bedroom Could you help me / suggest me ideas? I like / love / prefer … I would like my bedroom to be … No, I don't think that's a good idea… I would prefer ...	**Rôle B** What is your favourite colour / star / sport…? What colour(s) would you like on the walls? How do you imagine the furniture (bed, chair, armchair, table, shelves)? You could paint … / install … / buy a new …

UNIT
7

TÂCHE FINALE **Présenter une startup à partir d'une *mind map***

EOC – A2+

From Startups to Giants

1 2 Track 15 **Listen and fill in the information you hear.**

City: ....

State: ....

Nickname of the area: ....

2 2 Track 16 **Match the activities and the names of the companies. Listen and check.**

a. They provide video streaming. (..............................)

b. They design and sell mobiles, PCs and apps.
(..............................)

c. They help people buy and sell goods worldwide.
(..............................)

d. They help people connect by sharing personal media.
(..............................)

BREAK IN VIDEO

 # vidéo
Welcome to Silicon Valley – 1'01''
foucherconnect.fr/18tten25

a. The scene takes place in:
☐ San Francisco ☐ New York

b. You can be:
☐ 20 years old ☐ 90 years old
to start a company

c. The energy in Silicon Valley is:
☐ dangerous ☐ intoxicating

Keys to Success

Activity A An Easy-to-Use App

Starting point of the product
He partly missed a .... game.

Founder / Company
Brad Griffith / ....

Product
An app to find .... for live events at the .... price in a few seconds.

Slogan
"The seats you want, at the price you want, right now."

Market
.... + ...

Target[1]
The .... that uses smartphones.

Number of investors / Funding[2]
.... / ....

Using the app
With the ...., I can find the perfect seats. As soon as I've paid, the app displays the .... And now, all I need to do is transfer them to my friends via ....

1. *cible* ; 2. *financement*

1 Track 17 Listen and complete the information in the mind map.

Activity B A Smart Product

CONSUMER ELECTRONICS SHOW, LAS VEGAS

The product
- ☐ Intelligent sportswear
- ☐ Intelligent footwear
- ☐ Smartshoe
- ☐ Digitsole

Karim Oumnia, the founder of Digitsole

Demonstration
- He has connected the shoe to a:
  ☐ watch ☐ smartphone app
- Through the app, he has:
  - ☐ heated the shoe
  - ☐ cooled down the shoe
  - ☐ changed its height[1]
  - ☐ tightened[2] the shoe
  - ☐ loosened[3] the shoe

1. *hauteur* ; 2. *resserré* ; 3. *desserré*

2 Track 18 Listen to the interview and tick the correct information.

Activity C The Latest Safety Feature

BLAZE LASERLIGHT IN LONDON

Based in London, Blaze is a company which creates innovative urban cycling products. They have developed Blaze Laserlight, which improves visibility by broadcasting the image of a bicycle six metres in front of the rider.

→ **Emily Brooke**, co-founder and CEO[1]: *"A study has revealed that 75% of the cyclists in London feel safer[2] while riding with Blaze Laserlight."*

BLAZE LASERLIGHT IN NEW YORK CITY

Motivate is the company which operates the public bicycle sharing[3] system serving New York City.

→ **Jay Walder**, CEO: *"Motivate has seen 37 million trips completed since 2013, with few serious injuries[4]. We have installed the Blaze Laserlight on 250 bikes to make New York riders more visible to drivers and pedestrians."*

1. *Chief Executive Officer* = PDG ; 2. *plus en sécurité* ; 3. *vélos en libre-service* ; 4. *blessure*

3 Read the document and complete the grid.

Company	Blaze	Motivate
Headquarters	....	....
Provides[1]	....	The public bicycle sharing system in NYC
CEO	....	....
Device[2]	Blaze Laserlight	....
Advantages of the device	Improves visibility by broadcasting the image of a bicycle six metres in front of a rider.	....

1. *fournit* ; 2. *système*

4 2 Track 19 **Listen to the interview and tick the right answers.**

a. When did Emily Brooke have the idea of creating Blaze Laserlight?

☐ When a bus driver couldn't see her when cycling down a busy street in London.

☐ When she nearly had an accident with a cyclist.

b. What has Blaze Laserlight changed for cyclists?

☐ They can go faster.

☐ They are more visible to other road users.

NOW ACT

5 **Use the mind map on page 134 to record an oral presentation of the startup.**

FOCUS

a. A study **has** reveal**ed** that cyclists feel safer.

b. I **haven't seen** a shoe like that before.

c. **Have** you invent**ed** the shoe of the future? Yes, I have. / No, I haven't.

- *Le temps employé se construit avec* **have** *au présent* + *part. passé*
- *Il s'agit du :* ☐ *prétérit* ☐ *present perfect*
- *Les événements sont :*

☐ *passés, datés et terminés*

☐ *non terminés ayant un rapport avec le moment où l'on parle*

Training ex. 3, 5

A Startup to Watch

Activity D A Woman-Run Startup

Emily Weiss, founder and CEO of Glossier.

In New York City, the beauty startup Glossier has grown from a beauty blog to a beauty brand. Since its launch[1] in 2014 by Emily Weiss, Glossier, Inc. has already earned $40 million in venture capital funding[2].

Like many brands, Glossier relies largely on word of mouth to attract new customers, especially on social media. Every day, they post photos and share sayings[3] on Instagram. But what sets Glossier apart is that the beauty editors have already tried all the products. Moreover, they constantly communicate with real Glossier users, who tell Glossier what types of products they would like to see. In her team, Emily Weiss wants people who can collaborate with others, solve problems and feel excitement for the brand.

Glossier hasn't developed in Europe yet but it's a startup to watch as there has never been a better time for this startup to develop.

1. *lancement* ; **2.** *financement de capital-risque* ; **3.** *dictons*

1 **Read the text and underline the following information about the startup.**

name – type – headquarters – founder – founding date – funding

2 **Find the English for:**

a. *se développer* (§1): ....

b. *une marque* (§1): ....

c. *le bouche à oreille* (§2): ....

d. *résoudre des problèmes* (§2): ....

3 **Tick "Right" or "Wrong". Frame the sentences in the text to justify your answers.**

	Right	Wrong
a. Glossier uses social media to attract new customers.	☐	☐
b. At Glossier, the employees have never tried the products they sell.	☐	☐
c. Any person can become a Glossier team member.	☐	☐

NOW ACT

4 **Say in French what you have understood from the text.**

FOCUS

a. **Glossier has already earned $40 million.**

b. **Glossier hasn't developed in Europe yet.**

c. **There has never been a better time.**

- *Les mots en rouge sont des :* ☐ *adverbes* ☐ *adjectifs*
- *Quel est le temps employé ?* ....

Training ex. 4

VIDEO TIME 7

Israeli Startups in NY

 # vidéo
Israeli Startups are HIRING in NY! – 2'02''
foucherconnect.fr/18tten26

Step 1 **Before watching the video.**

1 Look at the picture and the title of the video. Make hypotheses about its topic.

....

....

....

....

....

Step 2 **Watch the whole video.**

2 Tick the correct information.

a. The video is an advertising film[1] to recruit:
☐ employees ☐ a CEO ☐ a co-founder

b. The video was shot in:
☐ Los Angeles ☐ Israel ☐ Manhattan

c. All the people speaking are:
☐ employees ☐ customers[2]
☐ co-founders or CEOs

d. On the various signs, it says:
☐ We're selling ☐ We're hiring
☐ We're buying

1. *spot publicitaire* ; 2. *clients*

Step 3 **Watch the video up to 0:32.**

3 Underline the right startups.

a. Adam Singolda is the founder and CEO of (*Datorama / Taboola / Via*).

b. Ran Sarig is the CEO and co-founder of (*WeWork / Innovid / Datorama*).

c. Michal Tsur is the co-founder and president of (*HYPR / Kultura / Via*).

d. Daniel Ramot is the co-founder of (*Oliver / Taboola / Via*).

4 Circle the sentence Guy Franklin says.

a. Thousands of Israeli startups…

b. Millions of Israeli startups…

c. Hundreds of Israeli startups…

…are expanding from Tel Aviv to New York and looking for new talents to grow their business.

HELP!

figure out comprendre
fulfill réaliser (un rêve)
grow* faire grandir
hire employer
niche ciblé
out of the box original
a subscription un abonnement

Fiche VIDEO TIME 7 *Israeli Startups* complète disponible en téléchargement

UNIT 7 Training

#exo
foucherconnect.fr/18tten27

IN TUNE

A 2 Track 20 Écoutez la prononciation des mots suivants puis répétez-les.

fond /ɒ/ found /aʊ/ fund /ʌ/

B 2 Track 21 Écoutez les mots (a à j) et cochez le son que vous entendez.

	a	b	c	d	e	f	g	h	i	j
/ɒ/										
/aʊ/										
/ʌ/										

1 Placez les mots dans la grille en vous aidant du nombre de lettres.

3 letters
CEO
use

4 letters
apps

5 letters
smart

6 letters
career
design
target

7 letters
founder
funding
startup

8 letters
founding
investor
software

Vocabulary

Nouns

an app(lication) une appli(cation)
a career une carrière
a Chief Executive Officer (CEO) un PDG
a co-founder un(e) cofondateur(trice)
a device un appareil, un système
a founder un(e) fondateur(trice), un(e) créateur(trice)
funding le financement
goods des marchandises
headquarters un siège social
an investor un investisseur
a purpose un but
software un/des logiciel(s)
a target une cible

Verbs

cool down refroidir
design concevoir
found fonder, créer
grow* augmenter, développer
heat chauffer
launch lancer
provide fournir
share partager

Adjectives

challenging stimulant
creative créatif
innovative novateur
smart (US) intelligent

Adverbs

already déjà
never jamais
not… yet pas encore

2 2 Track 22 **Écoutez et complétez les légendes des photos ci-dessous.**

a. Silicon valley is the .... of the world's largest high-tech corporations.

b. The .... I have always wanted is a mini Bluetooth speaker.

c. Steve Jobs was the ...., chairman and CEO of Apple Inc.

d. The engineers have designed the .... of a new car.

3 **Complétez les phrases à l'aide du participe passé des verbes entre parenthèses.**

a. The founder of the startup has .... a whole new concept. (create)

b. We've .... a 3D printer. (buy)

c. Has he .... the CEO? (inform)

d. I haven't .... about your idea. (think)

4 **En fonction du sens, complétez les phrases avec « already », « yet » et « never ».**

a. I've .... used Google Glass because I'm not very keen on it.

b. Machines haven't totally replaced humans ....

c. As they've .... invested in this startup, they want results.

5 **Utilisez les éléments pour former des énoncés au *present perfect*.**

a. The high-tech sector / recruit / many employees.

....

....

b. No / I / receive / any new software.

....

....

c. So many startups / come / to the show.

....

....

Language TIPS

Le *present perfect* « *have* + participe passé »

sujet	have	participe passé
I / You / We / You / They	have haven't	verbe régulier → V + *ed*
He / she / it	has hasn't	verbe irrégulier → *voir liste sur rabat*

→ Exprimer une relation entre un fait passé et la situation présente

Up to now, I have worked on this project.
Jusqu'à présent, j'ai travaillé sur ce projet.

He has made a prototype for the show.
Il a fait un prototype pour la présentation.

→ Faire le bilan de ce que l'on a fait jusqu'à présent

Have you been to the show? Yes, I have. / No, I haven't.
Es-tu allé à la présentation ? Oui / Non.

Les adverbes de temps

→ Exprimer l'idée de « jusqu'à présent »

Already, never, not... yet

They have already / never tested the device.
Ils ont déja / n'ont jamais testé l'appareil.

They haven't launched production yet.
Ils n'ont pas encore lancé la production.

FINAL TASK 7 Present an Innovative Startup

SCENARIO Dans le cadre de l'organisation d'un forum des métiers, vous devez présenter une startup de votre choix.

Étape 1 Réaliser une *mind map* sur une startup EE – A2+

- Sélectionnez un domaine qui vous intéresse (la mode, la technologie, le sport, etc.).
- Choisissez une startup qui présente un produit innovant dans ce domaine. Quelques exemples : AirB'nB (hébergement), Uber (transport), Birchbox (beauté), Dropbox (technologie), Housekeep (nettoyage), Running Heroes (sport), Magic Leap (réalité augmentée), etc.
- Cherchez des informations pour réaliser une *mind map* en vous inspirant de la trame proposée ci-dessous.
- Cherchez des photos et insérez-les.

Vous pouvez noter quelques éléments sur la *mind map* (noms propres, dates, chiffres) mais ne rédigez pas de phrases complètes.

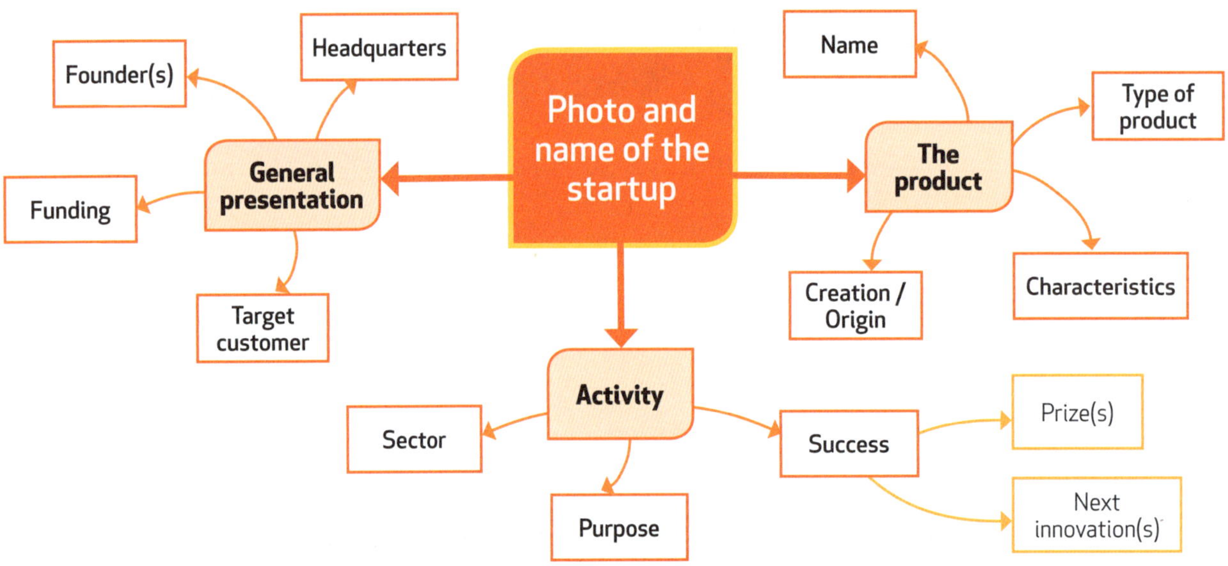

Étape 2 Présenter une startup EOC – A2+

- Pour chaque item, préparez, soit oralement, soit par écrit, deux ou trois énoncés qui correspondront aux photos sélectionnées ou aux éléments que vous voulez présenter.
- Entraînez-vous à présenter oralement l'entreprise choisie en utilisant seulement la *mind map* réalisée.
- Faites ensuite votre présentation devant la classe.

mon bilan UNIT 7

	J'ai réussi à…	--	-	+	++
EOC	Décrire une startup à l'aide d'une *mind map*				
CE	Comprendre un article sur l'évolution d'une startup				
CO	Comprendre une présentation d'entreprise				
EE	Réaliser une *mind map* sur une startup				
EOC	Présenter une startup				

S'exprimer à partir d'une *mind map*

CCF PREP 13

PARTIE 1 EOC

LET'S TRAIN!

1 Track 23 **Écoutez la présentation et soulignez ce que vous entendez.**

(*I'm going to / I would like to*) present a famous startup called Snapchat. (*I've chosen / I've decided*) to use a (*slide show / mind map*) to present this company. To organize my ideas and remember my plan, (*I've chosen / I've inserted*) some pictures and I've written a few (*details / pieces of information*).

(*I've split / I've divided*) my presentation into three parts (*named / entitled*) The Company, The Product and Its Use.

First of all, let me (*tell you / give you*) some facts about the company. Snap Inc. is a technology and social media company (*based / located*) in Los Angeles. In 2017, funding is about $3 billion. (*In the photo / In the picture*), we can see the founders of Snapchat: Evan Spiegel, Bobby Murphy and Reggie Brown. I would like to (*focus on / concentrate on*) the fact that they were students at Stanford University when they created Snapchat.

YOUR TURN!

2 **Sélectionnez certaines expressions parmi celles proposées dans l'exercice 1 pour poursuivre la présentation du produit et de son utilisation en utilisant les informations de la *mind map*.**

CCF PREP 14

PARTIE 2 EOI

Répondre à des questions sur une startup à partir d'une *mind map*

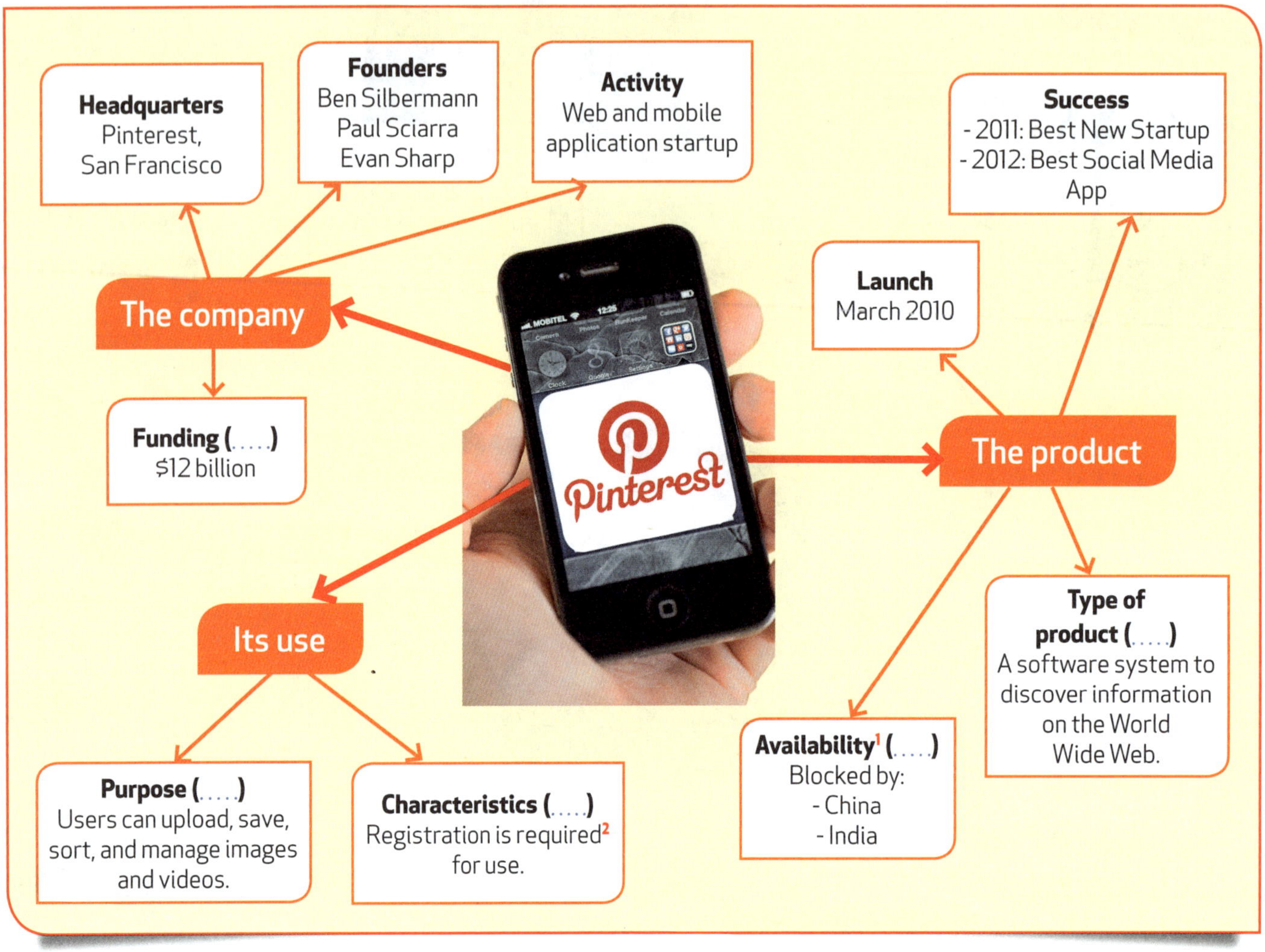

1. *disponibilité* ; **2.** *exigé*

1 Utilisez la *mind map* pour répondre aux questions suivantes.

a. What is the name of the company?

....

b. Is that also the name of the product?

....

2 2 Track 24 Écoutez les cinq questions enregistrées. Notez la lettre de la question dans la case adéquate puis répondez oralement.

YOUR TURN!

3 Préparez d'autres questions sur la *mind map* puis répondez aux questions de votre partenaire.

a. ....

b. ....

c. ....

d. ....

e. ....

f. ....

UNIT
8

TÂCHE FINALE Présenter une tribu amérindienne

EOC – B1

Native Americans

2. Geronimo (1829 – ....)
Tribe: ....

3. Sitting Bull (.......... – 1890)
Tribe: ....

1. Tecumseh
(.............. – 1813)
Tribe: ....

4. Quanah Parker (1845 – ....)
Tribe: ....

1 2 Track 25 **Listen and write the names of the tribes in the labels.**

Chiricahua Apache – Lakota Sioux – Shawnee – Comanche

2 2 Track 25 **Listen again and fill in the missing dates.**

3 **Match the actions and the chiefs (1, 2, 3, 4).**

- **a.** He defeated General Custer at Little Bighorn. .....
- **b.** He fought white American bison hunters. .....
- **c.** He wanted to ally the Native American tribes. .....
- **d.** He organised raids against white settlers*. .....

*colons

BREAK IN VIDEO

vidéo
Geronimo – 1'34''
foucherconnect.fr/18tten28

a. The video is: ☐ a documentary ☐ a trailer

b. In 1886, ☐ 59 Sioux ☐ 39 Apaches
were still fighting the US Army.

c. ☐ **The soldiers** ☐ **Americans**
were horrified by the details of the chase.

c. Geronimo became the symbol of:
☐ pillaging ☐ freedom of the American West.

Cultural Identity

Activity A Outfits and Weapons

1. a ....
2. a tomahawk
3. a rifle
4. a feather ....

5. a buckskin[1] ....
6. ....
7. cotton or woollen[2] ....
8. ....
9. ....

Some .... were very peaceful. Others had a .... spirit, ready to .... on the warpath[3].

Everyday clothes were appropriate for the .... conditions. Ceremonial clothes were made of .... and .... with beads[4].

1. *en peau de daim* ; **2.** *en laine* ; **3.** *sentier de la guerre* ; **4.** *perles*

1 2 Track 26 **Write the items from the list in the labels. Listen and check.**

tunic – belt – bow and arrows – jewellery – moccasins – headdress – dresses

2 **Orally describe the people on the photos.**

The man/woman/women in the left-hand/right-hand photo is/are wearing… / is holding…

3 2 Track 27 **Listen and complete the captions with the information you hear.**

Activity B Native Housing

4 2 Track 28 **Listen and tick "Right" or "Wrong".**

	Right	Wrong
a. Some tribes lived in homes called wigwams.	☐	☐
b. This home could be moved easily.	☐	☐
c. It could house 20 people.	☐	☐
d. Wigwams were built by men.	☐	☐

Activity C Spirits and Beliefs

A

B

C

D

5 Match the captions and the photos.

a. Native Americans offered prayers in religious ceremonies and sealed[1] peace treaties by smoking the peace pipe. (......)

b. Each warrior had to find his spirit animal when he came of age[2]. (.....)

c. For them, Wakan Tanka, the Great Spirit, was present in all things on Earth. (......)

d. They thought that the "medicine man" could invoke or appease the spirits. (......)

1. sceller ; 2. en devenant adulte

Activity D Ritual Dancing

6 2 Track 29 **Listen. Underline the wrong information and correct it.**

a. Tribes performed rain dances, particularly in the north-east of the USA. (......................................)

b. The rain dance was performed in mid- to late June. (......................................)

c. Dancers wore feathers and turquoise to symbolize wind and the desert. (......................................)

d. Only men could perform the rain dance. (......................................)

NOW ACT

7 **Use the elements on page 135 to give a description of one of the men and talk about his actions.**

FOCUS

a. **The warrior is holding his weapons.**

b. **The women are wearing cotton dresses.**

- *Ce temps sert à :* ☐ *décrire une action ou une image*
  ☐ *parler d'un événement habituel*
- *Le présent en –ing se construit avec* .... *au* .... + ... –ing

c. **The medicine man could invoke the spirits.**

d. **Each warrior had to find his spirit animal.**

- *Dans quel énoncé la forme soulignée signifie-t-elle :*
  – « *devait* » : ☐ c ☐ d
  – « *pouvait* » : ☐ c ☐ d

Training ex. 2, 3, 4, 5

Native Americans Today

Activity E — Off-Reservation Life

TRADITIONS STILL ALIVE

In the 1950s, the US Government's assimilation policies isolated Native Americans from their communities. Many of them were relocated from their land into urban areas. Orphans were placed into the homes of white families.

Chah-tah Gould is one of few[1] Ohlone tribal members left.

The Ohlone went nearly extinct after generations of slavery and colonization by Spain, Mexico, and the US. "Today, a lot of city Natives grow up in foster care and get into gangs. On reservations, they grow up around their culture. But here, you know, to be cool, you start drinking and smoking, all this other stuff[2]," Chah-tah says. "Out here you have to deal with the American-type life: taxes, jobs, everything like that."

Today, many Native Americans live off-reservation, in urban environments. Poverty remains one of the most challenging[3] aspects to contemporary urban Indian life. However many centers and programs help them to stay in the Native community and a lot of Natives do know their culture and even the ones who are into gangs, still go to powwows[4].

1. *l'un des quelques/rares* ; **2.** *et tout le reste* ; **3.** *éprouvant* ; **4.** *rassemblement festif*

1 Read the text and answer the questions.

a. Where do most Native Americans live today? ....

b. Who is Chah-tah Gould? ....

2 Find in the document the English for:

a. *transférer (§1) :* ....

b. *orphelin (§1) :* ....

c. *famille d'accueil (§2) :* ....

d. *dans les réserves (§2) :* ....

3 Tick "Right" or "Wrong".

	Right	Wrong
a. The Ohlone were completely exterminated.	☐	☐
b. Many Native American teens belong to gangs.	☐	☐
c. Many Natives in cities have poor living conditions.	☐	☐
d. The people have lost their traditions.	☐	☐

4 Underline in the text what 1950s' assimilation policies consisted of.

NOW ACT

5 Read the text about powwows on page 136 and say in French what you have understood.

VIDEO TIME 8

Crazy Horse Monument

vidéo
Crazy Horse Memorial Set to Be the World's Largest Monument - 2'08''
foucherconnect.fr/18tten29

Step 1 Before watching the video.

1 Look at the picture above and read the title of the video. Then make hypotheses about the topic of the video in English or in French.

....

....

....

Step 2 Watch the whole video.

2 Tick the correct information.

a. The video is a documentary about a monument to Crazy Horse, a Native American:
☐ chief ☐ horse ☐ medicine man

b. The sculptor at the origin of the project was:
☐ Kaleb Ziolkowski ☐ Monique Ziolkowski
☐ Korczak Ziolkowski

c. Tom Hanson, the journalist, works for:
☐ CNN ☐ Channel Four ☐ Channel One News

HELP!

blast faire exploser
a carving une sculpture
complete achever
a crew une équipe
a decade une décennie
outstretched tendu
oversee* superviser
take* shape prendre forme

Step 3 Watch the video up to 0:22.

3 Underline the correct information.

a. (*October / November / December*) is Native American Indian Heritage Month.

b. The Crazy Horse Memorial is named for the famous (*Cherokee / Crow / Lakota*) warrior.

c. It will be the (*highest / largest / deepest*) mountain carving in the world when it's complete.

Step 4 Watch the video from 0:23 to 0:50.

4 Complete the script.

A monument to a Native American .... Crazy Horse is slowly taking shape high above the .... in South Dakota. For nearly ...., crews have been blasting .... of rock off the mountain. Sculptor Korczak Ziolkowski began construction here in .... His work on Mount Rushmore drew the attention of .... Henry "Standing Bear", who invited him to design a memorial for ....

Fiche VIDEO TIME 8 *Crazy Horse Monument* **complète disponible en téléchargement**

UNIT 8

Training

#exo
foucherconnect.fr/18tten30

IN TUNE

A 2 Track 30 **Écoutez la prononciation des lettres « ea » dans les mots suivants et répétez-les.**

east /iː/ leather /e/ great /ei/ hear /ɪə/ wear /eə/

B 2 Track 31 **Placez les mots de la liste dans la colonne adéquate. Écoutez et vérifiez.**

bear – peace – near – feather – break – weather – please – fear – pear

/iː/	/e/	/ei/	/ɪə/	/ eə/

1 Complétez la grille de mots croisés à l'aide des illustrations.

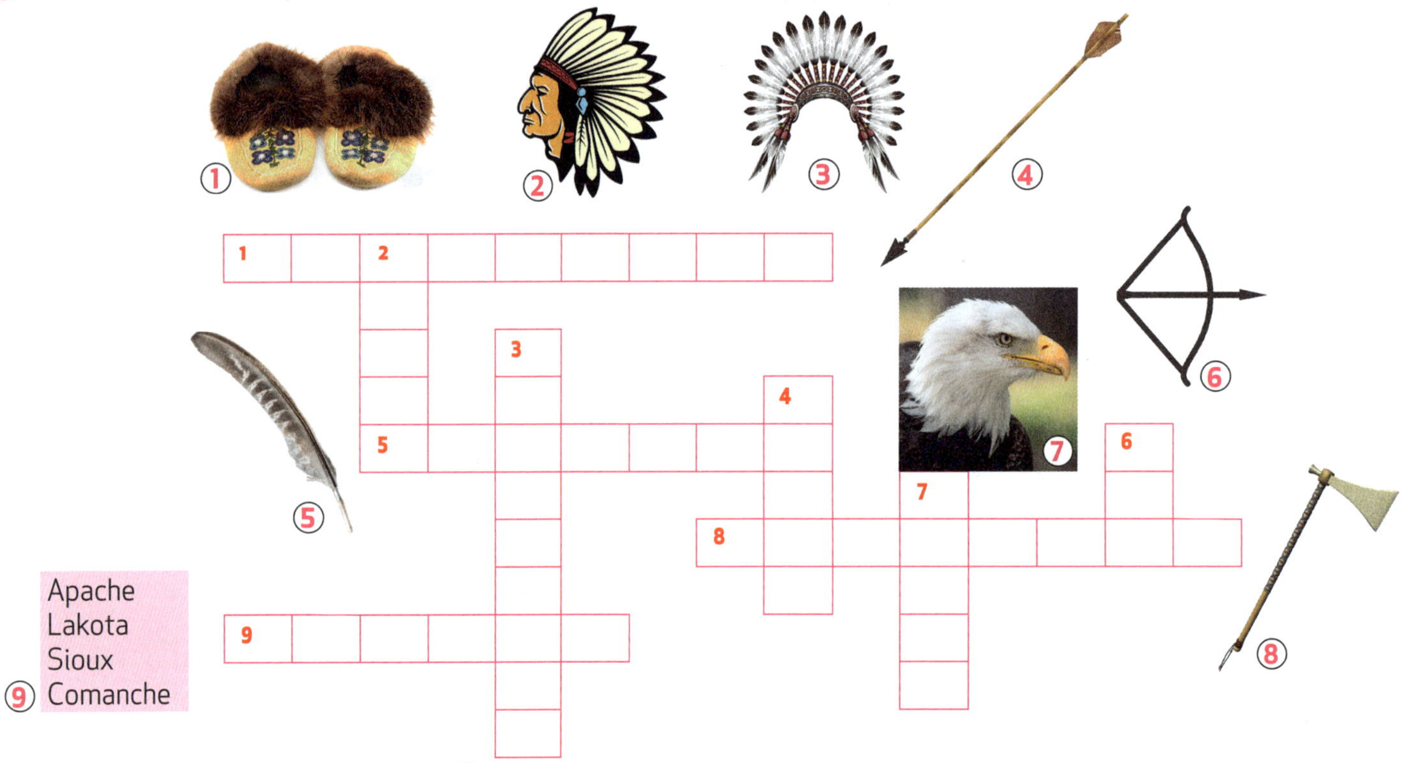

Vocabulary

Nouns
an arrow une flèche
a belief une croyance
a bow un arc
a feather une plume
a headdress une coiffe
a hunter un chasseur
a medicine man un sorcier
an outfit une tenue
a peace pipe un calumet de la paix
a reservation une réserve
a rifle un fusil
a settler un colon
a spirit un esprit
a tribe une tribu
the warpath le sentier de la guerre
a warrior un guerrier
a weapon une arme

Verbs
appease apaiser
belong to appartenir à
defeat vaincre
fight* combattre, se battre
invoke invoquer
move déplacer
perform réaliser

Adjectives
buckskin en peau de daim
peaceful pacifique

Others
in the background à l'arrière-plan
in the foreground au premier plan
in the middle ground au plan intermédiaire

2 2 Track 32 **Écoutez et complétez les légendes des photos ci-dessous.**

a.

Here, the warrior .... a bison.

b.

In this photo, the women .... dinner.

c.

This Apache warrior .... his horse.

d.

These warriors .... the soldiers.

3 **Complétez les phrases en conjuguant les verbes entre parenthèses au présent en *-ing*.**

a. The warrior ..... only .... the convoy. *(watch)*

b. This year, the dancers .... a war dance. *(perform)*

c. What .... they .... at the moment? *(do)*

d. Right now, the medicine man .... not .... but he .... to the spirits. *(fight - pray)*

e. Tonight I'm going to a fancy-dress party*. I .... a Native American costume. *(wear)*

**une soirée/fête costumée*

4 **Utilisez les mots entre parenthèses pour compléter les réponses aux questions.**

a. Is she making fire? *(cook)*

No, she isn't, but ....

b. Are they fighting enemies? *(dance)*

No, they aren't, but ....

c. Is he fishing? *(hunt)*

No, he isn't, but ....

d. Are you reading a thriller? *(watch a western)*

No, I'm not, but ....

5 **Complétez les énoncés à l'aide de « *had to* » ou « *could* ».**

a. The women had many tasks to do. For example, they .... gather firewood.

b. The situation was risky. Some tribes were not peaceful at all and .... dig up the hatchet at any time.

c. The Apaches were not gardeners. They .... hunt to find food.

d. With his incantations, the medicine man .... force the rain to fall.

e. To seal a peace treaty, Indians and white men .... smoke the peace pipe.

Language TIPS

Le présent en *-ing* : *be* + V *-ing*

Sujet	*Be* au présent	Verbe en *-ing*
I	am (not)	wearing
He / she / it	is (not)	
We / You / They	are (not)	

→ **Décrire une action en cours**

In the photo, the Sioux chief is wearing a wonderful headdress. *Sur la photo, le chef Sioux porte une magnifique coiffe.*

He isn't singing. *Il ne chante pas.*

What is the medicine man doing? *Que fait le sorcier ?*

Could

→ **Exprimer une capacité, une possibilité au passé.**

They could ride horses. *Ils savaient monter à cheval.*

They could track an animal for hours. *Ils pouvaient pister un animal pendant des heures.*

Had to

→ **Exprimer une obligation au passé.**

They had to hunt to survive. *Ils devaient chasser pour survivre.*

FINAL TASK 8 Present a Native American Tribe

SCENARIO

Votre classe organise une exposition interactive sur le thème des indiens d'Amérique du Nord. Vous devez réaliser une affiche accompagnée d'un enregistrement pour présenter une tribu amérindienne.

Étape 1 Trouver des informations pertinentes à propos d'une tribu CE – A2+

- Choisissez l'une des tribus de la carte.
- Cherchez des informations pour compléter la fiche.

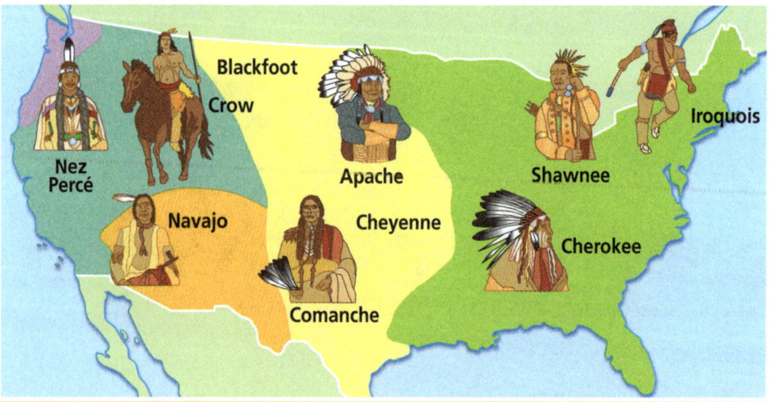

Name of the tribe: …………………………………………		
Way of living	**Traditions**	**Historical facts**
Place of living: ………………	Religion and beliefs: ………………	Famous people: ………………
Type of houses: ………………		Main battles: ………………
Type of clothes: ………………	Ceremonies: ………………	Other: ………………
2 or 3 weapons: ………………		

Étape 2 Réaliser une affiche sur une tribu EE – A2+

- Sélectionnez plusieurs photos représentatives de l'histoire, des traditions et du mode de vie de cette tribu.
- Utilisez les informations et photos sélectionnées pour réaliser une affiche sur la tribu choisie.

Étape 3 Présenter la tribu EOC – B1

- Entraînez-vous à présenter la tribu choisie à partir de votre affiche avant de vous enregistrer.
- Vos affiches seront exposées et votre enregistrement sera accessible à tous grâce à un QR code présent sur votre affiche ou des mp3 mis à disposition.

Tuto création QR code : www.unitag.io/fr/qrcode

mon bilan UNIT 8

	J'ai réussi à…	− −	−	+	++
EOC	Présenter et décrire une personne				
CE	Comprendre un article sur l'assimilation d'un peuple				
CO	Comprendre un reportage sur un mémorial				
EE	Réaliser une affiche sur une tribu				
EOC	Présenter une tribu amérindienne				

UNIT 8

Présenter un tableau

CCF PREP 15

PARTIE 1 EOC

LET'S TRAIN!

Charles Marion Russell, *Water for Camp*, 1892.

1 2 Track 33 **Écoutez et soulignez les éléments que vous entendez.**

a. In 1892, Charles Marion Russell, a cowboy artist, painted *Water for Camp* (depicting / representing) the everyday life of Native American women on a (Sioux / Crow) Indian encampment. This (photo / painting) shows Native American women drawing water from the (lake / river) and bringing it to the camp.

b. In the foreground, we can see two women drawing water from the river with a bucket. They are wearing traditional (woollen / buckskin) clothes and feather earrings and they have (short / plaited[1]) hair.

c. In the middle ground, two women are (walking / running) back to the (wigwam / tepee) village.

d. In the background, (on the right-hand side / on the left-hand side), a group of women are preparing some food. In the distance, on the right-hand side we can make out[2] the (plains / mountains) of Montana.

e. The painting (reflects / throws back) a peaceful atmosphere showing how all the members of the (tribe / community) are working together at the everyday tasks of the camp.

1. *natté* ; 2. *deviner*

2 **Placez les éléments écrits en couleur autour du document.**

YOUR TURN!

3 **Décrivez le tableau ci-contre.**

Paul Kane, *Native American Encampment on Lake Huron*, 1845.

CCF PREP 16

PARTIE 3 CE

Comprendre un article sur un musée

Indianapolis, Indiana: The Eiteljorg Museum of American Indians and Western Art

I'm a big museum person and was delighted to hear that there was a museum dedicated to Native Americans – their culture and art – on the western edge of downtown Indianapolis, in White River State Park. [...]

The architecture of the buildings is stunning. The museum was commissioned[1] by an Indianapolis businessman, Harrison Eiteljorg, to educate, inspire and promote a better understanding of art from the western part of the United States. His other objective was to build a museum that paid homage to Native American culture, art, and history. [...]

The Eiteljorg is the only museum of its kind in the Midwest and houses art, artifacts[2], exhibits and documents from most of the Native American tribes in North America with a concentration on those from the current United States. [...]

Like many Americans, I have Native American roots - my great grandmother was one of the Indian children taken away from her family and sent to a boarding school[3] in Philadelphia. [...]

I felt connected to our history, to our land and to our people. By studying our Native American heritage we learn who we are as a people.

Regina Fraser, Pat Johnson, *www.huffingtonpost.com*, October 22, 2016.

1. *commander* ; **2.** *objets* ; **3.** *internat*

Répondez aux questions en français.

1. Quel est le sujet du document ?

....

2. Qui a créé ce musée et pourquoi ?

....

....

3. Que peut-on voir dans ce musée ?

....

....

4. Pourquoi la journaliste est-elle si intéressée par ce musée ?

....

....

5. Qu'a-t-elle ressenti après avoir visité le musée ?

....

....

The Two Faces of Ireland

Culture **CLICK 4**

Number of inhabitants: about ....

Currency: ....

Independence from the United Kingdom: ....

Government: Parliamentary

....

Member of the EEC[1] since

....

1. *Communauté économique européenne (CEE).*

Number of inhabitants: about

....

Currency: ....

....

Government: constitutional monarchy

1 2 Track 34 **Listen and fill in the labels and the missing information.**

Belfast's murals

2 2 Track 35 **Listen and tick "True" or "False".**

	True	False
a. 'The Troubles' is the name of a conflict in Northern Ireland.	☐	☐
b. The conflict started in the 1970s and finished in 1998.	☐	☐
c. It was an armed conflict between the Unionists and the Nationalists.	☐	☐
d. The Unionists wanted independence from the UK.	☐	☐
e. The IRA was founded in 1919.	☐	☐

Quiz

1 The other name of the Republic of Ireland is:
a. Iceland ☐
b. Eire ☐
c. Ulster ☐

2 The other name of Northern Ireland is:
a. Iceland ☐
b. Eire ☐
c. Ulster ☐

3 The official languages are:
a. English ☐
b. Irish ☐
c. Scottish ☐

4 Ireland's national holiday is:
a. St Patrick's Day ☐
b. Independence Day ☐
c. Poppy Day ☐

5 The emblem of Ireland is:
a. a salmon ☐
b. a shamrock ☐
c. a leprechaun ☐

6 Guinness is an Irish:
a. cake ☐
b. tea ☐
c. beer ☐

7 Irish coffee is:
a. coffee and tea ☐
b. coffee and ice cream ☐
c. coffee, cream and whiskey ☐

8 A traditional Irish breakfast is:
a. bacon and eggs ☐
b. black pudding, bacon and eggs ☐
c. cereal and tea ☐

9 Eithne Ni Bhraonain is the real name of the Irish singer:
a. Dana ☐
b. Enya ☐
c. Sinead O'Connor ☐

10 A traditional Irish musical instrument is:
a. the violin ☐
b. the bagpipe ☐
c. the harp ☐

2 Track 36 **Listen and check.**

Your score: … /10

The title of the song *Sunday Bloody Sunday* by the band called U2 refers to a particular day in Irish history: Sunday January 30th, 1972, when Irish Catholics decided to demonstrate in the streets of Derry in Northern Ireland. They wanted the same opportunities as the Protestant community. English troops tried to break up the demonstration; they opened fire on the unarmed and peaceful civilians and shot 13 of them. This event shocked many countries in the world.

3 Read the text and answer the questions.

a. Why did Irish Catholics demonstrate on January 30th, 1972?

....

b. Were the demonstrators armed or violent?

....

c. How did the British army react?

....

Now go on the Web and listen to the song *Sunday Bloody Sunday* by the band called U2.

4 Listen to the song *Zombie* by the Cranberries and complete the script (2'43 → 3'05).

#audio foucherconnect.fr/18tten40

It's the same old theme
Since nineteen-sixteen
In your head, in your head, they're still ....
With their ...., *and their* ....
And their ...., *and their* ....
In your head, in your head, they are ....

The words you've added relate to: ☐ freedom ☐ violence ☐ war ☐ peace

Comment décrire une image

FICHE **AP4**

Méthode

1 Observez la nature du document.

Dites s'il s'agit d'un tableau, d'une photo, d'une BD, d'une affiche ou d'un dessin.

2 Décrivez ce que vous voyez... ♫A

- portrait, paysage, scène de campagne, de ville, de nuit…
- le nombre de personnages, leur position, le lieu…

3 ... puis prêtez attention aux détails. ♫B

Observez l'arrière-plan, les petits détails.
Utilisez le vocabulaire de description de l'image et soyez le plus précis possible.

4 Recherchez et utilisez les informations.

Intéressez-vous à l'artiste, au contexte historique, au mouvement artistique.

5 Émettez des hypothèses. ♫C

Imaginez les relations entre les personnages, leurs actions, le lieu…
Utilisez les expressions adéquates.

6 Exprimez votre avis et vos émotions sur l'image. ♫D

Apprenez quelques expressions pour parler de vos goûts et de vos sentiments.

Vos outils

#audio foucherconnect.fr/18tten31

♫A Caractériser l'image

landscape *paysage*
portrait *portrait*
seascape *paysage marin*
cartoon *image*
painting *peinture*
character *personnage*

♫B Situer dans l'espace

in the background *à l'arrière plan*
in the foreground *au premier plan*
at the top *en haut* **at the bottom** *en bas*
on the left *à gauche* **on the right** *à droite*
in the top right hand corner *en haut au coin à droite*
in the centre/middle *au centre/milieu*

♫C Formuler des hypothèses

Maybe *Peut-être que*
It is possible that *Il est possible que*
We can imagine *On peut imaginer que*
We may suppose *On peut supposer que*

♫D Exprimer des sentiments

I love it *J'adore*
I like it very much *J'aime beaucoup*
What I don't like is that… *Ce que je n'aime pas, c'est que…*
It reminds me of *Cela me rappelle*
It makes me feel happy/sad/excited/romantic *Cela me rend heureux/triste/enthousiaste/romantique*

● Écoutez attentivement les expressions ci-dessus et entraînez-vous à les répéter.
Puis essayez de mémoriser au moins huit expressions que vous utiliserez au verso.

FICHE **AP 4**

Comment décrire une image

Entraînez-vous !

Activité 1 Décrire et analyser un tableau

Pierre-Auguste Renoir, *Le bal du Moulin de la Galette*, 1876, 131 x 175 cm, Musée d'Orsay, Paris.

A. Faites une description aussi complète que possible de l'œuvre ci-dessus.

Type of document	....
Description	....

B. Faites des recherches sur Pierre-Auguste Renoir et son mouvement artistique.

....

....

C. Prolongez votre travail en émettant des hypothèses sur les relations entre les personnages.

....

....

D. Exprimez votre point de vue et vos sentiments.

....

....

Activité 2 Faire une présentation orale

Présentez une image de votre choix à la classe en suivant les étapes de l'activité 1.

UNIT 9

TÂCHE FINALE Présenter un aspect des années 1920

EOC – B1

The Roaring Twenties

1 Track 37 **Match the definitions and the words. Listen and check.**

Gangsters	○	○	Period when Americans could not drink alcohol.
Prohibition	○	○	Women's movement against alcohol and speakeasies[1].
The Roaring Twenties	○	○	Criminals who smuggled[2] alcohol.
Women's Temperance Movement	○	○	Nickname for the 1920s.

1. bars clandestins ; 2. faire de la contrebande

2 **Write the caption under the pictures.**

Gangsters - Roaring Twenties – Prohibition – Women's Temperance Movement

BREAK IN VIDEO

 # vidéo
The Untouchables - Trailer – 3'37''
foucherconnect.fr/18tten32

a. The document is:
☐ an ad ☐ a trailer

b. Robert De Niro plays:
☐ Al Capone ☐ "Lucky" Luciano

c. The action takes place in:
☐ New York ☐ Chicago

d. The title of the film is:
☐ *The Incorruptible* ☐ *The Untouchables*

EOC– A2+

Historical Background

Activity A Major Events

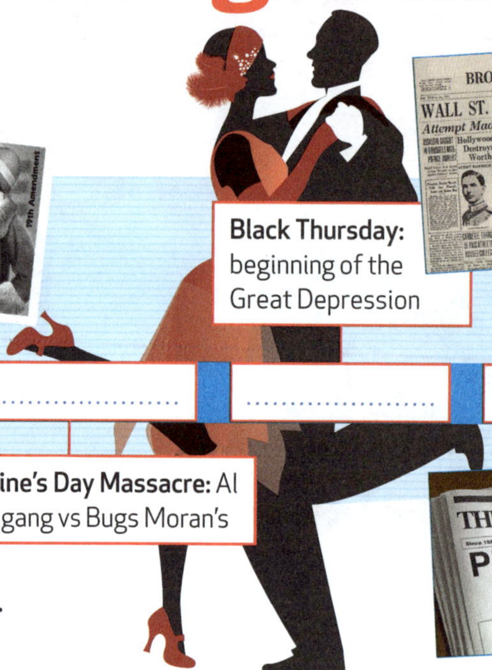

- 1893: Anti-Saloon League
- January 1919: ....
- August 1920: ....
- ....: St Valentine's Day Massacre: Al Capone's gang vs Bugs Moran's
- ....: Black Thursday: beginning of the Great Depression
- ....

1 Track 38 Listen and fill in the blanks in the timeline.

2 Track 39 Tick the right definitions. Then listen and check.

a. Black Thursday was: ☐ New York stock exchange[1] crash ☐ Paris stock exchange crash

b. The St Valentine's Day Massacre was a battle between: ☐ cops and gangs ☐ two rival gangs

c. The Great Depression was: ☐ a worldwide economic boom ☐ a worldwide economic collapse[2]

1. bourse ; 2. effondrement

Activity B Gatsby: an Ambivalent Character

The novel tells of the fall of Jay Gatsby, who is in love with Daisy, herself .... to another man. It is set in America when Prohibition was at its peak. Gatsby has a .... past and is famous for throwing huge .... He represents rich America that listened to jazz music and .... alcohol despite the ban[3]. He also embodies[4] ....

The story is seen through the eyes of Nick Carraway, Gatsby's .... F. Scott Fitzgerald, who .... the novel in 1925, was an American author. The book has been .... three times into films:
- 1926: a .... movie;
- 1974: Gatsby is played by Robert Redford;
- 2013: Leonardo Di Caprio plays the hero.

3. interdiction ; 4. incarne

3 Complete the text with the following words.

wrote – parties – neighbour – troubled – married – silent – drank – business – adapted

4 Track 40 Listen and tick the right answer.

a. Mary loves the latest *Great Gatsby* adaptation because it is full of: ☐ colours ☐ odours

b. She likes: ☐ blues music ☐ jazz music

c. The story is: ☐ captivating ☐ fascinating

d. The story captures perfectly: ☐ the happy side ☐ the decline of the Twenties.

Activity C Famous Gangsters

Al Capone
City: ....

Enoch Lewis Johnson
City: ....

"Lucky" Luciano
City: ....

5 2 Track 41 **Listen and write the names of the cities of these notorious gangsters.**

6 2 Track 42 **Listen and tick the right answers.**

a. Gangsters were in charge of: ☐ bootlegging ☐ education
b. The "untouchables" were: ☐ gangsters ☐ policemen
c. Enoch Johnson inspired a: ☐ TV character ☐ book character
d. "Lucky" Luciano is considered the: ☐ brother ☐ father of modern organized crime.

7 2 Track 43 **Listen and tick "Right" or "Wrong".**

	Right	Wrong
a. Gangsters were all born in Italy.	☐	☐
b. Al Capone and Lucky Luciano were friends.	☐	☐
c. Enoch Johnson was a political figure in Atlantic City.	☐	☐
d. Al Capone went to jail for tax evasion.	☐	☐

NOW ACT

8 2 Track 44 **Listen and fill in the grid about the Saint Valentine 's Day Massacre on page 137.**

FOCUS

a. Their businesses ended on the day <u>when</u> Prohibition failed.

b. F. Scott Fitzgerald, <u>who</u> wrote the book, was an American author.

c. The places <u>where</u> organized crime developed the most were the big cities.

● *Parmi les pronoms relatifs soulignés, dites lequel fait référence :*

- au lieu : ....
- à la date : ....
- à la personne : ....

Training ex. 4, 5

The Downsides of the 'Twenties'

Activity D Why Did Prohibition Fail?

Prohibition ended with the repeal of the Volstead Act on December 5, 1933 and the ratification of the Twenty-First Amendment. This put an end to a thirteen-year experiment on banning alcohol. The Temperance League reformers and the "drys" —those who did not drink and were in favour of Prohibition— failed to convince the American people. The "wets" —those who drank and thus were against Prohibition— won the war over alcohol consumption.

Prohibition failed for many reasons. First of all, due to the limited number of agents, it was impossible for them to do their job properly and arrest smugglers (or bootleggers). Secondly, the size of the country itself was an issue. The country was too large and the agents too few. Moreover, those agents were not paid enough and some of them took bribes from criminals.

The third reason was that during Prohibition the number of crimes rose. Organized crime and gangland murders were more common during Prohibition than before. Organized crime increased in big cities where mobsters used to have their businesses.

To finish, the crash of the stock market left many people unemployed. Some thought that the reopening of alcohol industries would bring jobs to many Americans.

1 Find in the document the English for:

a. *révocation* (§ 1) : ....

b. *expérience* (§ 1) : ....

c. *réformateurs* (§ 1) : ....

d. *contrebandier* (§ 2): ....

e. *pot-de-vin* (§ 2) : ....

f. *truand* (§ 3): ....

2 Read the text and answer the questions.

a. Who were the "wets"?

....

b. What were the problems with prohibition agents?

....

c. What happened to organized crime?

....

3 Underline in the text the last reason why Prohibition failed.

NOW ACT

4 Explain in French what you have understood.

FOCUS

Organized crime increased in big cities where mobsters used to have their businesses.

- *L'énoncé exprime :*

☐ *une habitude dans le passé*

☐ *une habitude au présent*

Training ex. 3

VIDEO TIME 9

Ken Burn's Prohibition

 # vidéo
Ken Burn's Prohibition
- 2'08''
foucherconnect.fr/18tten33

Step 1 Before watching the video.

1 Read the title of the video and make hypothesis about the subject.

....

....

....

....

Step 2 Watch the whole video.

2 Underline the correct answers.

a. The channel is (*PBS* / *CNN*).
b. This is (*an ending* / *a trailer*).
c. This video is (*a film* / *a documentary*).

Step 3 Watch the video up to 0:18.

3 Choose the right answers.

a. Prohibition was:
☐ expected ☐ a surprise
b. It turned citizens into:
☐ criminals ☐ thugs
c. Prohibition changed the nature of American:
☐ society ☐ democracy

Step 4 Watch the video from 0:18 to 0:28.

4 Underline "Right" or "Wrong".

a. You can see happy people. Right Wrong
b. The music is rap. Right Wrong
c. Prohibition was a great idea. Right Wrong

Step 5 Watch the video from 0:28 to 1:04.

5 Fill in the blanks with the words: *small – middle – man – job – wets – family*.

a. It was a struggle between .... towns and big cities, the .... and the drys, with the whole country caught in the ....
b. You drank to show that you were a ...., but you get drunk and all of a sudden you can't provide for your ...., you can't do your ....

HELP!

ban interdire
citizens des citoyens
pray prier
preposterous absurde
roar rugir
struggle lutter

Fiche VIDEO TIME 9 *Ken Burn's Prohibition* complète disponible en téléchargement

UNIT 9

Training

#exo foucherconnect.fr/18tten34

IN TUNE

A 2 Track 45 **Écoutez la prononciation du « h » dans « *prohibition* » et « *honest* » et répétez.**

B 2 Track 46 **Écoutez et classez les mots suivants en fonction de la prononciation de la lettre « h ».**

	hour	exhausted	him	alcohol	who	honesty
« h » muet						
« h » aspiré						

1 **À l'aide des définitions, remplissez la grille de mots croisés.**

Down
1. Nickname for the 1920s: the xxx Twenties
2. Synonym of "mobster"
4. Illegal bar

Across
3. Period of time when alcohol was banned
5. Transport alcohol illegally

2 **Utilisez le vocabulaire pour compléter les phrases.**
parties – illegal – failed – exchange – stock

a. During Prohibition, it was .... to buy alcohol.
b. On October 24, 1929, the New York .... crashed.
c. In the 1920s, wealthy people had a lot of ....
d. In the end, Prohibition ....

Vocabulary

Nouns
alcohol de l'alcool
a bootlegger un contrebandier
a crash un krach, une faillite
a downside un inconvénient
a gangster un criminel
a party une fête
a speakeasy un bar clandestin
a stock exchange une bourse
tax evasion la fraude fiscale

Verbs
ban interdire
drink* boire
fail échouer
repeal révoquer
smuggle faire de la contrebande

Adjectives
illegal illégal
roaring rugissant

3 2 Track 47 **Remettez les éléments des phrases dans l'ordre. Puis écoutez pour vérifier.**

a. people / before Prohibition / drink / alcohol / used to

....

....

b. used to / gangsters / alcohol / smuggle

....

....

c. fight / women / against / bars / some / used to

....

....

4 **Soulignez le pronom relatif qui convient.**

a. Gangsters (*when/who*) were famous were arrested after Prohibition.

b. Prohibition was the time (*when/where*) alcohol was forbidden.

c. Distilleries (*who/which*) produced alcohol had to stop.

d. In big cities (*where/whose*) there was a lot of smuggling, there were lots of gangsters.

e. Speakeasies were the places (*where/when*) people could drink illegally.

5 **Complétez par le pronom relatif qui convient.**

a. People .... didn't drink alcohol were called "drys".

b. The place .... organised crime was the most developed was Chicago.

c. The day .... the stock market crashed is known as Black Thursday.

6 **Indiquez si chacune des affirmations suivantes est vraie (Right) ou fausse (Wrong).**

	Right	Wrong
a. Al Capone was never arrested for bootlegging.	☐	☐
b. Gangsters' stories have inspired films and television.	☐	☐
c. Gangsters' illegal activities stopped after Prohibition.	☐	☐

Language TIPS

Les pronoms relatifs

→ ***Where*** **(le lieu)**

America is the country where there was Prohibition.

L'Amérique est le pays où il y a eu la Prohibition.

→ ***When*** **(le moment)**

1919 was the year when Prohibition started.

1919 est l'année où la prohibition a commencé.

→ ***Who*** **(la personne)**

Look! That's the man who arrested Al Capone.

Regarde ! C'est l'homme qui a arrêté Al Capone.

Used to

Some people used to drink illegally during Prohibition.

Certaines personnes avaient l'habitude de boire illégalement pendant la prohibition.

FINAL TASK 9 Present an Aspect of the Roaring Twenties

SCENARIO Vous êtes invité à la webradio de votre lycée pour présenter un aspect de l'Amérique des années 1920.

Étape 1 Compléter une fiche concernant un aspect des années 1920 EE – A2+

- Choisissez un des aspects suivants :
  - Speakeasies
  - Women's Temperance Movement
  - Jazz music
  - St Valentine's Day Massacre
  - Black Thursday
- Cherchez sur Internet les informations sur l'aspect choisi pour compléter la fiche ci-dessous.
  Vous pouvez consulter les sites suivants :
  - www.history.com
  - www.infoplease.com/encyclopedia

Title:	
People	....
Places	....
Dates	....
Important facts or information	....
Surprising information	....

Étape 2 Présenter l'aspect choisi EOC – B1

- Utilisez les éléments de votre fiche pour produire des énoncés.
- Entraînez-vous à les répéter afin que votre présentation soit fluide.
- Enregistrez votre présentation pour sa diffusion.

mon bilan UNIT 9

	J'ai réussi à…	−−	−	+	++
EO	Présenter un événement majeur d'une chronologie				
CE	Comprendre les causes de l'échec de la Prohibition				
CO	Comprendre les événements principaux de la Prohibition				
EO	Présenter un aspect des années 1920				

UNIT 9 Présenter un film

CCF PREP 17
PARTIE 1 EOC

LET'S TRAIN!

....
I am going to talk about the film *Gatsby*, directed by Baz Luhrmann. It is ....

....
We find the same characters as in the novel. Leonardo Di Caprio plays the .... of Gatsby and Carey Mulligan, Daisy.

....
The .... is the life of Jay Gatsby. He is a businessman who falls in love with Daisy, who is already married.
The story is told by a third character, Nick Carraway.

....
It was .... in May 2013.

....
I think it is a great .... of the Roaring Twenties.

1 2 Track 48 **Écoutez et complétez la présentation du film.**

2 **Donnez un titre à chaque partie.**
Release date – Conclusion – Introduction – Story line – Cast

3 2 Track 48 **Réécoutez et répétez cette présentation.**

YOUR TURN!

4 **Utilisez les éléments suivants pour faire une présentation du film *Angels With Dirty Faces*.**

- **Title:** *Angels With Dirty Faces*
- **Introduction:** A classic mobster movie
- **Actors:** James Cagney / Rocky Sullivan / Pat O'Brien / Jerry Connelly
- **Plot:** A priest tries to stop a gangster from corrupting a group of street kids.
- **Release date:** 1938
- **Conclusion:** A must-see

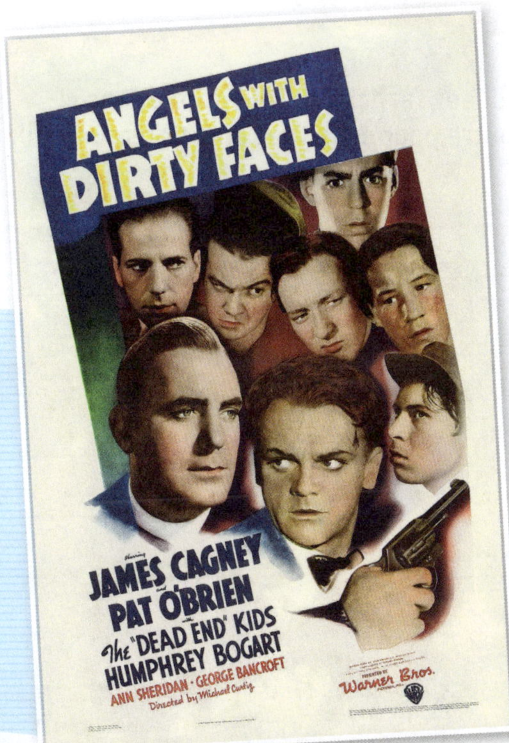

CCF PREP 18

PARTIE 2 EOI

Poser des questions sur la présentation d'un film

LET'S TRAIN!

MIDNIGHT IN PARIS

Actors:
Owen Wilson, Marion Cotillard

Plot:
While on a trip to Paris, an American screenwriter mysteriously goes back to the 1920s every day at midnight.

Opinion:
very emotional and poetic

Release date: 2011

Conclusion: a must-see

1 2 Track 49 Utilisez le poster du film et les informations ci-dessus pour répondre aux questions enregistrées.

a. ....

b. ....

....

....

c. ....

....

d. ....

....

e. ....

....

YOUR TURN!

2 Utilisez l'affiche et les informations ci-contre pour poser des questions sur le film.

a. ....

b. ....

c. ....

d. ....

e. ....

f. ....

....

....

....

Director:
Sergio Leone

Main actor:
Robert de Niro

Place:
America

Period:
20th century

Plot:
story of friendship between gangsters

Opinion:
greatest film ever made

UNIT **10**

TÂCHE FINALE → **Écrire un récit à suspense**

EE – B1

Thrilling Stories

Sherlock Holmes

Job: ....

Tasks: .... mysterious cases using .... and observation

Place of work: Baker Street, ...

Partner: ....

Annalise Keating

Job: lawyer and ....

Tasks: solve .... cases

Place of work: .... of America

Partners: five of her ....

1 **Look at the photos and say what you know about the two characters.**

2 2 Track 50 **Complete the labels with the words below. Then listen and check.**

students, Dr Watson, detective, murder, United States, solve, logic, London, teacher.

3 **Match the tasks of a detective (a-b-c-d) and the French equivalents.**

a. examine crime scenes **c.** analyse clues
b. question suspects **d.** take photos of footprints

1. *analyser les indices (.....)*
2. *photographier les empreintes de pas (.....)*
3. *examiner les scènes de crime (.....)*
4. *interroger les suspects (.....)*

BREAK IN VIDEO

 # vidéo
Detectives and Criminals Investigators Job Overview – 1'08''
foucherconnect.fr/18tten35

a. **The video explains the professional:**
☐ tasks
☐ status of detectives and criminal investigators.

b. **They can:**
☐ give first aid ☐ investigate a murder
☐ take part in a fight ☐ stop a fight
☐ patrol an area to prevent crime

c. **Police officers can be promoted detectives after:**
☐ 1 to 3 ☐ 3 to 5 years' experience.

Masterpieces of Suspense

Activity A Initial Situation

Information about the author

....

....

....

back cover

'Julia, it's me. I need you to .... me .... Please, Julia. It's important…'

....

In the last days before her ...., Nel Abbott called her .... Julia didn't pick up her phone, ignoring her plea[1] for ....
Now Nel is .... They say she ....
Julia is .... So afraid. Of her long-buried[2] memories, of the Old Mill…
And most of all she's afraid of the ...., and the .... they call the Drowning Pool…

synopsis

1. appel ; 2. enfouis depuis longtemps

1 Look at the document and fill in the empty labels with: *name of the author, front cover, book title, extract.*

2 Track 51 Listen and complete the back cover. Then explain what you have understood.

Activity B Thrilling Events

a — Sound effect # ....

b — Sound effect # ....

c — Sound effect # ....

3 Track 52 Listen to the sound effects from the movie *The Birds* by Hitchcock and match them to the pictures.

4 Match the descriptions to the corresponding scenes.

a. After the attack of a man by birds, petrol was spilling* all around when someone lit a cigar. ○
b. The children were singing when crows gathered around the building. Soon after, they were forced to run away. ○
c. The heroine, Melanie, hid from the birds. ○

○ A. the school attack scene
○ B. the gas station scene
○ C. the phone booth scene

* se répandait

Activity C Solving Cases

....

....

....

5 **Match the pictures and their titles:** *murder – house burglary – child kidnapping.*

6 2 Track 53 **Listen and answer the questions.**

a. When was the young boy kidnapped? ....

b. When did the burglar enter the house? ....

c. When was the old lady murdered? ....

7 2 Track 54 **Complete with** *compare, draw*, examine, take*, question, use* **in the preterite. Listen and check.**

a. The police officers .... the young boy's friends and .... an Identikit picture[1] of the man. Then they found him very quickly.

b. The detective .... fingerprints[2] and .... them with those of well-known robbers. The robber was arrested the following week.

c. The federal agents .... DNA fingerprinting to find the murderer. They also .... his motives; in fact, the criminal was his son, he was interested in his mother's money.

1. *portrait robot* ; **2.** *empreintes digitales*

NOW ACT

8 **Look at the cartoon on page 136 and write sentences to describe what happened.**

....

....

....

....

....

....

....

....

FOCUS

a. **The burglar entered the house while the family was sleeping.**

b. **Petrol was spilling all around when someone lit a cigar.**

- *La structure des formes verbales soulignées est : Be au .... + V..........*
- *Ce temps exprime :*
  - ☐ *un événement présent*
  - ☐ *une activité qui était en cours dans le passé*
- *Comment traduire :*
  - *- pendant que ?* ....
  - *- quand ?* ....

Training ex. 3

The Queen of Suspense

Activity D *Death on the Nile*, by Agatha Christie

Parker Pyne Investigates

Lady Grayle, 48 and immensely rich, and her husband Sir George Grayle were on a private cruise[1] on the Nile with their niece, Pamela, and their staff – a nurse, Miss MacNaughton, and a private secretary, Basil. There was also another passenger on board, Parker Pyne, a private detective. Lady Grayle asked him to investigate because she suspected her husband of poisoning her. Then, in turn, a few days later, the nurse asked for Parker Pyne's help because she also suspected Lady Grayle to be the victim of poisoning. The following night, Lady Grayle died of convulsions after having drunk a beverage prepared by her nurse and Sir George. Pamela first thought her aunt[2] had poisoned herself but poison was later found in Sir George's pockets. In the end, after investigating, the detective discovered that Basil had a love affair with Lady Grayle but decided to murder her because he had fallen in love with her niece.

1. *faire une croisière* ; **2.** *tante*

1 Match the characters and their roles in the short story *Death on the Nile*, written by Agatha Christie:

Lady Grayle	O	O the niece
Sir George	O	O the secretary
Pamela	O	O the victim
Basil	O	O the victim's husband
Parker Pyne	O	O the nurse
Miss MacNaughton	O	O the detective

2 Find in the document the English for:

a. *une infirmière* : ....

b. *à bord* : ....

c. *enquêter* : ....

d. *empoisonnement* : ....

e. *une boisson* : ....

f. *assassiner* : ....

3 Underline in the text the reason of the crime.

4 Write the names of the characters who are speaking.

a. 'I want to know whether or not my husband is poisoning me': ....

b. 'I have come to suspect that Lady Grayle is being poisoned': ....

c. 'I found a packet of strychnine in the pocket of his dinner jacket': ....

d. 'So you know all about it. You damned interfering nosy parker!': ....

NOW ACT

5 Complete in French the 5 steps of the story (page 137): initial situation – disruptive event – following events – resolution – final situation.

FOCUS

a. Pamela **first** thought that Lady Grayle was poisoned.

b. **A few days later**, she discovered he was a detective.

c. **The following night**, she died.

- *Ces mots servent à* ☐ *marquer la chronologie* ☐ *indiquer la cause ou la conséquence*
- *Quel(s) mot(s) signifie(nt)* :

- *la nuit suivante* : ....
- *quelques jours plus tard* : ....
- *d'abord* : ....

Training ex. 4

VIDEO TIME 10

Wind River

 # vidéo
Wind River Official Trailer (2017) – 2'35''
foucherconnect.fr/18tten36

Step 1 Before watching the video.

1 Look at the picture above. Give words you expect to hear in this trailer.

....

....

....

2 Make a hypothesis about what happens.

....

....

....

....

....

Step 2 Watch the whole video.

3 Tick the correct elements.

a. The victim is: ☐ a teenage boy
☐ a teenage girl

b. Jane Banner is: ☐ an FBI agent
☐ a CIA agent

c. Cory Lambert is: ☐ a police officer
☐ the person who found the dead body

Step 3 Watch the video up to 0:11.

4 Answer the questions.

a. Who can you see?

....

b. What is she doing?

....

c. Where and when does the scene take place?

....

Step 4 Watch the video from 0:12 to 0:26.

5 Tick the correct information.

a. Wind River is the name of:
☐ an Indian reservation
☐ an American state

b. It is: ☐ easy
☐ difficult to reach this area

HELP!

backup du soutien, du renfort
a clue un indice
hunt chasser
a reservation une réserve

Fiche VIDEO TIME 10 *Wind River* complète disponible en téléchargement

UNIT 10 Training

\# exo
foucherconnect.fr/18tten37

IN TUNE

A 2 Track 55 **Écoutez ces différentes façons de prononcer la lettre « a » en anglais et répétez.**

/ɔː/ call - /aː/ partner - /ae/ kidnap - /ei/ agent -/ə/ husband

B 2 Track 56 **Classez les mots selon la prononciation de la lettre « a ».**

man – draw – case – bath – negotiator – examine – cast – analyse – water – attack

[ɔː]	[ae]	[ei]	[ə]	[aː]

1 Entourez 10 mots appartenant au champ lexical du thriller.

F	I	N	G	E	R	P	R	I	N	T
I	N	V	E	S	T	I	G	A	T	E
K	M	D	E	T	E	C	T	I	V	E
M	I	G	A	W	V	S	N	L	B	T
U	M	D	Z	G	A	N	A	T	C	X
R	T	Q	N	S	I	N	R	E	D	R
D	Y	L	D	A	I	T	P	K	E	D
E	C	E	M	M	P	S	S	B	Y	Y
R	R	L	I	N	U	R	B	E	Z	T
T	B	R	U	S	G	O	X	R	V	G
L	C	N	D	E	R	A	N	S	O	M

Vocabulary

Nouns

a burglary un cambriolage
a character un personnage
a DNA fingerprint une empreinte ADN
a fight une bagarre
a firearm une arme à feu
jewellery des bijoux
a murder un meurtre
a neighbour un voisin
a ransom une rançon
a twist un renversement de situation

Verbs

choke (s')étrangler, (s')étouffer
draw* an identikit picture dresser un portrait-robot
investigate enquêter
keep* watch faire le guet
kidnap kidnapper
patrol patrouiller
prevent empêcher
shout crier
take* fingerprints relever des empreintes
wait for attendre

Adjectives

safe sûr, sécurisé
stressed tendu
well-known bien connu

2 2 Track 57 **Complétez la 4e de couverture de *All by Myself, Alone* de Mary Higgins Clark avec :**

ship, husband, rich, necklace, dead, expert, missing, eighty-six-year-old, arrested

Écoutez et vérifiez.

Celia Kilbride was a jewelry .... and her ....-to-be was .... just before their wedding. She decides to leave on a cruise ....—the *Queen Charlotte*.

On board she met .... Lady Emily Haywood, "Lady Em". Immensely ...., Lady Em was wearing a priceless emerald ....

Three days later, Lady Em was found .... —and the necklace was ....

3 **Conjuguez les verbes au prétérit simple ou au prétérit en *-ing*.**

a. The police officers .... still .... for two weeks when another murder .... (*investigate / happen*)

b. He .... for his parents after school when a woman .... him. (*wait / kidnap*)

c. They .... a love affair while they .... for business. (*have / travel*)

d. The detective .... the crime scene when he .... a clue. (*observe / find*)

e. The suspect .... a window when the policemen .... him. (*break / see*)

4 **Soulignez le connecteur qui convient.**

a. (*First/Afterwards*) the child was kidnapped; (*several days earlier / then*) the kidnappers asked for a ransom.

b. (*A few days later / Tomorrow*), the investigators arrested the two kidnappers.

c. They had been seen by neighbours (*several days earlier / after*) in the district.

5 **Complétez le tableau en vous aidant d'un dictionnaire en cas de besoin.**

Nom	Adjectif	Verbe
fright (*la peur*)	frightening (*effrayant*)	frighten (*effrayer*)
an investigation (........................)	investigative (*d'investigation*)	.... (*enquêter*)
.... (*la mort*)	.... (mort)	die (.....................)
.... (*un kidnapping, un enlèvement*)	kidnapped (.....................)	.... (*kidnapper, enlever*)

Language TIPS

Les connecteurs

Marquer la chronologie

First *d'abord*

First of all *tout d'abord*

Then / afterwards *ensuite*

Finally / eventually / in the end *finalement*

Yesterday *hier*

Tomorrow *demain*

A few hours later/after *quelques heures plus tard/après*

Several days earlier/before *plusieurs jours plus tôt/avant*

The following night *la nuit suivante*

The day after *le lendemain*

The day before *la veille*

Le prétérit en *-ing*

Exprimer des actions en cours à un moment précis du passé : *was/were* + V-*ing*

Il se traduit en général par un imparfait.

The child was kidnapped while he was playing with his friends in the playground.

L'enfant a été kidnappé alors qu'il jouait avec ses amis sur l'aire de jeux.

What were they doing?

Qu'étaient-ils en train de faire ?

FINAL TASK 10

Write a Detective Story

SCENARIO

Vous participez à un concours d'écriture et devez rédiger un récit à suspense.
Celui-ci sera publié sur une plateforme d'écriture.

Étape 1 Compléter les fiches pour bâtir la trame de l'histoire EE – A2+

- Observez l'illustration ci-contre.
- À partir de l'illustration, imaginez le début de votre récit et complétez la fiche suivante.

Location: a supermarket car park / a public car park / other: ....
Time of day: in the morning / in the afternoon / in the evening / other: ....
Characters: Ms............, a British superintendant / Mr. ...., a private detective / ...., a robber / ...., a drug dealer / ...., a kidnapper / other: ....
Initial situation: ....

- Imaginez l'identité d'un personnage supplémentaire intervenant dans la suite de l'histoire.

Name: ....
Job: ....
Role: victim – witness – detective… **Relationship:** ....

- Imaginez les étapes suivantes de l'histoire.

Disruptive event: ....
Following events: ....
Resolution: ....
Final situation: ....

Étape 2 Rédiger un récit EE – B1

- En 100 mots minimum, relatez les événements au prétérit (simple et en *-ing*) en utilisant les éléments des fiches complétées ci-dessus. N'oubliez pas d'insérer des connecteurs logiques de temps. Utilisez un dictionnaire en ligne, et relisez bien votre histoire.
- Postez votre histoire sur une plateforme d'écriture (www.wattpad.com) ou sur l'ENT du lycée.

mon bilan UNIT 10

	J'ai réussi à…	−−	−	+	++
EE	Rédiger les étapes d'une histoire à suspense				
CE	Comprendre la structure d'une histoire policière				
CO	Comprendre la bande-annonce d'un film à suspense				
EE	Écrire une histoire à suspense				

UNIT 10

Décrire une affiche de film

CCF PREP 19

PARTIE 1 EOC

LET'S TRAIN!

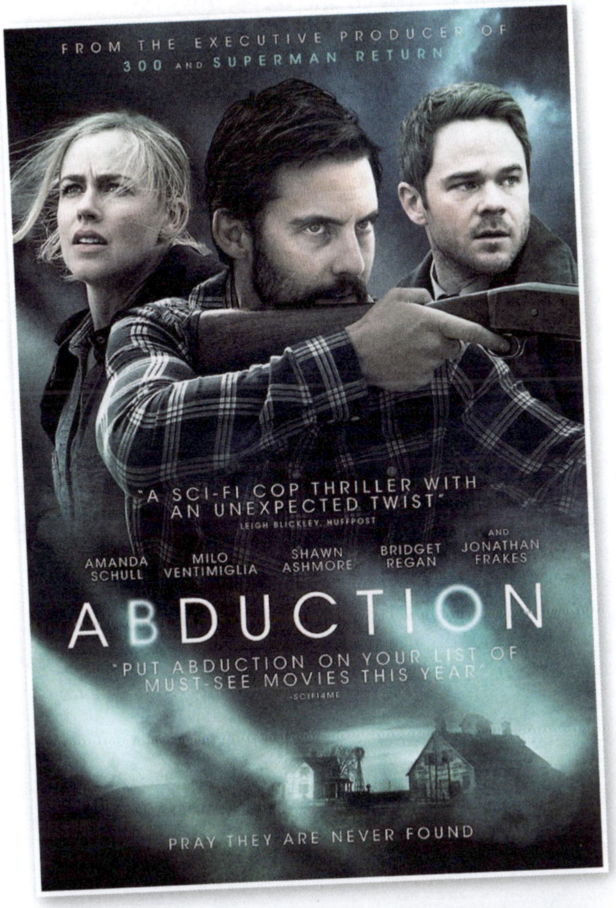

1 **Complétez en utilisant les éléments de l'affiche.**

a. This is the poster for the movie entitled .... produced by the producer of .... and ....

b. The actors are ....

c. The genre of the movie is ....

2 **Entourez les éléments qui conviennent pour décrire l'affiche.**

a. This is a black-and-white movie poster.

b. This is a colour movie poster.

c. There are three characters in the top part of the poster.

d. They are looking directly at the camera.

e. Each character is holding a firearm.

f. Two of them are looking around, maybe keeping watch.

g. In the bottom part of the poster, there are two houses.

h. The characters look relaxed and reassured.

i. The actors look stressed and worried.

j. The colours of the poster are dark and they contribute to the impression of mystery and danger.

3 **En utilisant les éléments des exercices 1 et 2, présentez oralement l'affiche.**

YOUR TURN!

4 **Présentez oralement cette affiche (ou celle de votre choix).**

Comprendre des avis de lecteurs

LET'S TRAIN!

Ten years after the high-profile kidnapping of two young boys, only one returns home.

A decade ago, kidnappers grabbed two boys from wealthy families and demanded ransom, then went silent. No trace of the boys ever surfaced. For ten years their families have been left with nothing but painful memories and a quiet desperation for the day that has finally miraculously arrived.

MARY BETH rated it ★★★★★ *May 19, 2017*

I have a book hangover after reading this book last night. I couldn't put it down and was up in the wee hours in the morning[1] finishing it! [...] The ending left me stunned but it was utterly perfect. Coben is an absolute master. His books have everything a good thriller should have. Can I rate this one higher than a five?

LARRY H rated it ★★★★★ *Mar 23, 2017*

Harlan Coben doesn't let the pace flag[2] in this book for one single second. There's some terrific action and suspense here, and you really don't know who you can trust. But there are some tremendous emotions displayed in this book, too, among all the characters. If you like great thrillers with strong plot[3] and character development, too, definitely pick this one up!

1. aux petites heures du matin ; 2. faiblir, ralentir ; 3. intrigue

Répondez aux questions en français.

1. Quel est le sujet du document ?

2. De quoi est composé le document ?

3. Que s'est-il passé il y a 10 ans dans le roman ?

4. Quelle est la situation dix ans plus tard ?

5. Pourquoi peut-on affirmer que la lectrice Mary Beth a été fascinée par le roman ?

6. Selon le lecteur Larry H, le succès du roman *Home* est-il seulement dû à l'intrigue ?

Self-Portraits

Culture CLICK 5

1

Name: Rembrandt Harmenszoon van Rijn
Title: *Self-Portrait with Two Circles*
Date of painting: ....- 1669
Pictorial movement: ......

2

Name: Claude Monet
Title: *Portrait with a Beret*
Date of painting: ....
Pictorial movement: ....

3

Name: Vincent Van Gogh
Title: *Self-Portrait with Bandaged Ear*
Date of painting: ....
Pictorial movement: ....

4

Name: Pablo Picasso
Title: *Self-Portrait*
Date of painting: ....
Pictorial movement: ......

5

Name: René Magritte
Title: *The Son of Man*
Date of painting: ....
Pictorial movement: ......

1 2 Track 58 **Listen and write the dates of the self-portraits in the labels.**

2 2 Track 58 **Listen again and write the letters corresponding to the style of the paintings.**

a. Impressionism b. Cubism c. Classicism d. Expressionism e. Surrealism

Quiz

1 The first self-portrait was by:
- **a.** Picasso ☐
- **b.** Jan van Eyck ☐
- **c.** Rembrandt ☐

2 Rembrandt painted:
- **a.** 50 self-portraits ☐
- **b.** 90 self-portraits ☐
- **c.** 150 self-portraits ☐

3 Van Gogh painted himself:
- **a.** 15 times ☐
- **b.** 40 times ☐
- **c.** 43 times ☐

4 Medieval self-portraits show the artist:
- **a.** at home ☐
- **b.** at work ☐
- **c.** sleeping ☐

5 Some artists used self-portrait for:
- **a.** fun ☐
- **b.** mockery ☐
- **c.** promotion ☐

6 The National Portrait gallery is in:
- **a.** Paris ☐
- **b.** New York ☐
- **c.** London ☐

7 Nowadays, a photographic self-portrait is called a:
- **a.** slide ☐
- **b.** selfie ☐
- **c.** film ☐

8 David Hockney's *Painting with Charlie* dates back to:
- **a.** 1899 ☐
- **b.** 1965 ☐
- **c.** 1995 ☐

9 *Triple Self-Portrait* is by:
- **a.** Norman Rockwell ☐
- **b.** Claude Monet ☐
- **c.** Parmigianino ☐

10 *Self-Portrait with Bandaged Ear* was sold for:
- **a.** $ 90 million ☐
- **b.** £ 110 million ☐
- **c.** $ 135 million ☐

2 Track 60 **Listen and check.**

Your score: … /10

Francis Bacon, *Self-Portrait, 1971*

3 2 Track 59 **Listen to the recording and tick the right answers.**

- **a.** Francis Bacon was born in: ☐ Berlin ☐ Dublin
- **b.** He was in conflict with: ☐ his father ☐ his mother
- **c.** He lived in: ☐ Madrid ☐ Paris
- **d.** Around 1944, he: ☐ cleaned ☐ destroyed his paintings.
- **e.** His self-portraits expressed: ☐ his anxiety ☐ his happiness

Pablo Picasso

Picasso (1888-1973) was one of the greatest and most influential artists of the 20th century. During his life, his style evolved. He painted or drew at least 14 portraits of himself between the ages of 15 and 89.
His self-portraits show his pictorial evolution. The first ones belong to the Realism movement but at the end of his life, his self-portraits are less and less realistic and are in the style of the Cubist pictorial movement.

Pablo Picasso, *Self-Portrait 90 Years Old*, June 28, 1972.

4 **Read the text and answer the questions.**

- **a.** When was Pablo Picasso born? ....
- **b.** When did he die? ....
- **c.** How many self-portraits did he paint? ....
- **d.** Which pictorial movement do his first paintings belong to? ....
- **e.** Which pictorial movement do his last paintings belong to? ....

Comment rédiger un texte court

FICHE **AP 5**

Méthode

1 Prenez en compte la situation d'énonciation.
Demandez-vous à qui le texte est destiné et qui le lira (votre famille, les élèves du lycée…).

2 Respectez les codes de mise en forme d'un écrit.
Tenez compte du type de document demandé (lettre, carte postale, article de presse, petite annonce, récit, dialogue, etc.) pour présenter le texte.

3 Suivez les consignes de rédaction.
Respectez le nombre de mots ou de lignes demandé.

4 Faites un plan.
Listez vos idées sous forme de mots-clés ou de phrases simples, puis ordonnez-les de façon logique.

5 Utilisez un dictionnaire papier ou en ligne.
Préférez le dictionnaire au traducteur. Cherchez les mots inconnus ou vérifiez leur orthographe.
(Voir Fiche AP2 page 53)

6 Respectez les règles de grammaire. ♫A
Faites des phrases courtes en respectant l'ordre des mots et les règles de grammaire. Évitez de traduire mot à mot. Utilisez les mots, les expressions et les structures étudiés en cours ou que vous connaissez.

7 Utilisez les temps appropriés. ♫B
Selon le sujet proposé, choisissez le temps le mieux adapté pour décrire, raconter, imaginer, etc. Utilisez un précis grammatical ou un site internet pour vérifier la construction des temps.

8 Établissez une chronologie. ♫C
Si le sujet vous le permet, situez l'action dans le temps en utilisant des mots de liaison qui expriment la chronologie des actions.

9 Utilisez des mots-outils.
Liez les idées en utilisant des connecteurs logiques qui expriment la cause, la conséquence, etc. pour structurer et complexifier votre écrit.

10 Relisez-vous !
Prenez quelques minutes pour relire et corriger votre texte.

Vos outils

 # audio foucherconnect.fr/18tten38

♫A Des règles de grammaire

> **Respectez la syntaxe** (sujet, verbe, complément).

> **Les adverbes** peuvent se placer en début de phrase ou avant un verbe : *It usually rains. D'habitude il pleut.*

> **Les adjectifs épithètes** se placent avant le nom auquel ils se rapportent : *the blue car* *la voiture bleue.*

> **Le verbe** suit directement le modal : *I can swim. Je sais nager.*

♫B Des temps appropriés

> Habitude : présent simple.

> Temps de narration au passé + indications datées : prétérit.

> Description dans le présent : présent en *-ing*.

> Description dans le passé : prétérit en *-ing*.

> Action passée dont le résultat dans le présent est important au moment de l'énoncé : *present perfect.*

> Action future : futur simple.

> Action hypothétique : conditionnel simple.

Site utile : www.anglaisfacile.com

♫C Des marqueurs de temps

> **first/at first** *d'abord*
then *puis* ;
after that *après* ;
next *ensuite*
later *on plus tard* ;
finally *enfin*

● **Utilisez les mots proposés dans le paragraphe C pour raconter brièvement ce que vous feriez si vous deveniez immensément riche.**

FICHE AP 5

Comment rédiger un texte court

Entraînez-vous !

Activité 1 Rédiger un courrier simple dans une situation courante

Dear Lucie,

My name is Mia, I'm 15. I'm studying French at school and I'm glad you are my pen friend. .... Maybe we could help each other.

I live in York. It's a very nice place with a lot of history and many cultural and sporting activities. ....

I only live in a small house. .... I've put all sorts of posters on the walls. What about your place? Do you live in a house or a flat? What's your bedroom like?

I'm sending you a photo of my family. You can see Mum and Dad with my brother Nate – that's short for Nathan. ....
Dad is a bus driver and mum is a waitress. What about your family? Can you send me a photo too?

Who's your favourite singer? I love Ed Sheeran. ....

I go to Huntington School. Fashion accessories are not permitted. .... I'm keen on business studies and I'm very good at ICT. .... Which subjects do you prefer? What do you want to be?

I have long, dark hair, brown eyes and I'm quite tall. I like swimming, reading love stories and I'm fond of fantasy films. ....

Oh, I forgot, our dog is a golden retriever called Dixie. Have you got a pet?
Write to me soon. Tell me about you and your family.

Love *Mia*

- **Replacez dans la lettre ci-dessus les énoncés suivants.**

We have to wear a plain black uniform. / *Perfect* is such a good song. /
It's also a very popular tourist destination. / On Tuesdays, I play badminton with my friends. /
He is 6 and he is very good at maths. / I want to be a graphic designer. /
However, my bedroom is nice and cosy. / I like French but it is difficult.

Activité 2 Décrire un lieu, une personne

- **Rédigez un paragraphe pour répondre aux questions de Mia en donnant des précisions sur l'endroit où vous habitez et quelques explications sur votre famille :**
ville/village, monuments, intérêts, type de maison/d'appartement, votre pièce préférée, etc.

Annexes

UNIT 1 Meet-ups

NOW ACT Page 10 exercise 5

UNIT 4 Ready for Work

NOW ACT Page 43 exercise 8

Annexes

UNIT 2 English Made Easy

NOW ACT Page 19 exercise 7

1/ First contact

2/ On the way to school

NOW ACT Page 20 exercise 5

PIZZAS

Margherita
Cheese Tomato €5.80

Four Seasons
Cheese Tomato Green peppers
Onions Mushrooms.............. €6.40

Hot Italian Hot
Cheese Tomato Onion
Spicy beef €7.60

UNIT 3 Welcome to London

NOW ACT > **Page 33** exercise 7 **Student A**

Step 1: Ask **Student B** questions about his/her landmark and fill in the form.

Name > ....

Location > ....

....

Date of opening > ....

Ticket price > ....

Opening times > ....

Number of visitors > ....

What to do / What to see >

....

....

....

....

Step 2: Answer **Student B's** questions.

Name > Orbit Tower

Location > Stratford (in Queen Elizabeth Olympic Park – East London)

Date of opening > 2014

Ticket price > Adult from £16.50 / Child from £10.50

Opening times > 10 am – 6 pm

What to do / What to see >

• Ride through the world's tallest and longest tunnel slide.

• Unique panorama of the city from the top of the tower.

Annexes

UNIT 3 Welcome to London

NOW ACT > Page 33 exercise 7 Student B

Step 1: Answer **Student A**'s questions.

Name > Harry Potter Warner Bros. Studios
Location > Leavesden – 30 km northwest of central London
Date of opening > 2012
Ticket price > Adult £69 / Child £64
Opening times > 10:00 am – 6:30 pm
Number of visitors > 6,000 a day
What to do / What to see >
- The Great Hall of Hogwarts Castle.
- Accessories from the films (Harry's Nimbus 2000, Hagrid's motorcycle…).
- Sets[1] from the films.

1. scènes/décors

Step 2: Ask **Student A** questions about his/her landmark and fill in the form.

Name > ....
Location > ....
....
Date of opening > ....
Ticket price > ....
Opening times > ....
What to do / What to see >
....
....
....
....

UNIT 5 Fabulous India

NOW ACT Page 57 exercise 9 Student A

Step 1: Ask **Student B** questions about Mumbai and fill in the form.

Fast Facts

Nickname: ....

State: ....

Area: .... / **Population:** ....

Local language: ....

The traditional Ganesh[1] festival

It is a festival in the honour of ....

....

....

There is ....

....

1. *Ganesh est le dieu le plus vénéré en Inde. Il est le dieu de la sagesse et du savoir.*

1869	....	....	2010
The city became .... for India's exports to Europe and the USA.	Indian film production began in the city.	Bombay was renamed Mumbai after the Hindu goddess Mumbadevi.	Mumbai became ....

Step 2: Use the information below to answer **Student B**'s questions about Kolkata.

Fast Facts

Nickname: City of Joy

State: West Bengal

Area: 185 km²

Population: 4.5 million

Local language: Bengali

The tradition of Jatras

Jatras are popular plays with loud music and splendid lighting.

They last four hours and are acted outdoors.

1690	1947	1970	2000
The British East India Company[1] developed trade in the city.	The city became the cultural capital of India.	Kolkata experienced an important economic decline.	IT[2] services, trade and industries started expanding again.

1. A trade company which seized control of the Indian subcontinent and ruled the beginnings of the British Empire in India ; 2. Information Technology

Annexes

UNIT 5 Fabulous India

NOW ACT Page 57 exercise 9 Student B

Step 1: Use the information below to answer **Student A**'s questions about Mumbai.

Mumbai

Fast Facts

Nickname: City of Seven Islands

State: Maharashtra

Area: 603 km^2 **Population:** 12.5 million

Local language: Marathi

The traditional Ganesh[1] festival

It is a festival in the honour of Ganesh, a god with an elephant's head. The festival lasts ten days. There is a parade and a lot of dancing and singing.

1. *Ganesh est le dieu le plus vénéré en Inde. Il est le dieu de la sagesse et du savoir.*

- **1869** – The city became a central port for India's exports to Europe and the USA.
- **1913** – Indian film production began in the city.
- **1995** – Bombay was renamed Mumbai after the Hindu goddess Mumbadevi.
- **2010** – Mumbai became the commercial capital of India.

Step 2: Ask **Student A** questions to fill in the form about Kolkata.

Kolkata

Fast Facts

Nickname: ....

State: ....

Area: .... **Population:** ....

Local language: ....

The tradition of Jatras

Jatras are ....

....

.... They last four hours and are acted ....

- **1690** – The British East India Company[1] developed .... in the city.
- **........** – The city became the cultural capital of India.
- **1970** – Kolkata experienced ....
- **........** – IT[2] services, trade and industries started expanding again.

1. A trade company which seized control of the Indian subcontinent and ruled the beginnings of the British Empire in India ; 2. Information Technology

UNIT 5

Fabulous India

NOW ACT Page 58 exercise 4

FIVE DISTINCT TRAITS OF BOLLYWOOD MOVIES

Bollywood! Beautiful, glamorous and a great way to spend some time with your family and friends. But what are the characteristics of any Bollywood movie?

1. Bollywood movies are long! When watching a Bollywood movie, you are transported to a completely different universe for at least[1] 3 hours. Indian filmmakers think that with a longer movie, the audiences will immerse themselves in the plot[2] and can better relate[3] to characters.

2. Bollywood movies are explosively colorful. Bollywood movies are known for their amazing costumes and neon[4] colors. Women are impeccably dressed in traditional saris, heavy jewelry, and copious makeup.

3. Bollywood movies have repetitive plots. The plot generally involves the protagonist (usually a male) falling in love with a rich aristocratic woman and after a lot of dancing, fighting, and crying, they are finally married. This type of story line has been used again and again in all different forms and scenarios to show that love conquers all.

4. Bollywood movies have a lot of music and dancing. Indian filmmakers use music and dance to make the movies more exciting. They also want the audiences to remember a movie very easily.

5. Bollywood movies always have a happy ending. Almost all Bollywood movies end with the protagonist and his lady love being married or two enemy families reuniting or the antagonist being punished for his wrongdoings[5].

1. *au moins* ; **2.** *intrigue* ; **3.** *s'identifier* ; **4.** *fluo* ; **5.** *méfaits*

UNIT 6

Smart Cities

NOW ACT Page 68 exercise 5

Read the summary and correct the wrong information.

The city of Los Angeles is facing many problems related to transport. It has been dubbed the second (..........) most congested city in America.

The city has both an issue with congestion and parking space.

Los Angeles has developed an app called "MUNI tel» (..) on which people can pay for tickets and rent bikes (..).

People have also a site called Fordgobike.com to rent taxis. (..)

San Francisco city and some students are currently working on an app of car-sharing.

Annexes

UNIT 7 From Startups to Giants

NOW ACT Page 81 exercise 5

Starting point of the product
An app to check soldiers' health

Product
The UP4 system: a connected wristband and a smartphone app

Product

Target
Everyone, but especially for fitness people

Jawbone

Its use

Using the UP app
The app tracks how you sleep, move, eat and burn calories to give you advice.

Company

Headquarters
San Francisco

Founders
Alexander Asseily
Hosain Rahman

Activity
Wearable* technology

Number of investors
14
Funding $165 million

* portable, mettable

UNIT 1 Meet-ups

NOW ACT Page 9 exercise 9

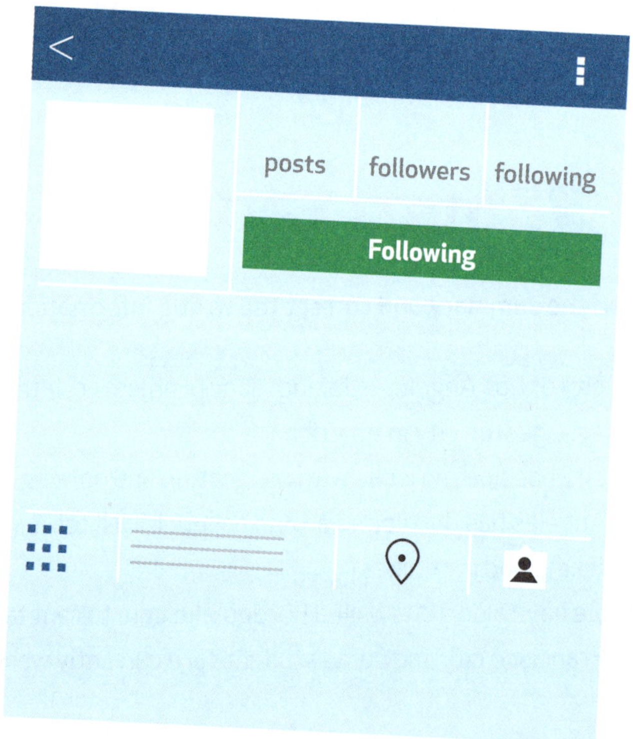

UNIT 8

Native Americans

NOW ACT Page 91 exercise 7

Warrior
Tribe: Chiricahua Apache
Place: Arizona
House: hut

Medicine man
Tribe: Cree
Place: Canada and Montana
House: tepee or wigwam

Medicine man
Tribe: Paiute
Place: Nevada and Oregon
House: wickiups

Warrior
Tribe: Black Foot
Place: Montana
House: tepee

Annexes

UNIT 8 Native Americans

NOW ACT Page 92 exercise 5

Kevin Kingbird, Don Kingbird and eight other singers of the Battle River group will sing the first and the last song of the day, which means they will probably be at the Rushmore Plaza Civic Center Arena up to 12 hours a day.

Kevin Kingbird said: "We select the songs carefully. We want to get a good rhythm, something to dance to, and something with some soul."

Don Kingbird said they brought a lot of old songs from Red Lake, Minn., and all the songs the members of their group have composed along the way.

"This sort of gathering brought the different people together to share news of marriages, deaths, births and life before breaking for winter. And it continues today,» he said.

Don said: "Look! The grass dancers are representing the movement of wind through the grass."

"Powwows are still practised today and our culture is still alive," Kevin said.

UNIT 10 Thrilling Stories

NOW ACT Page 115 exercise 8

UNIT 9 The Roaring Twenties

NOW ACT Page 105 exercise 8

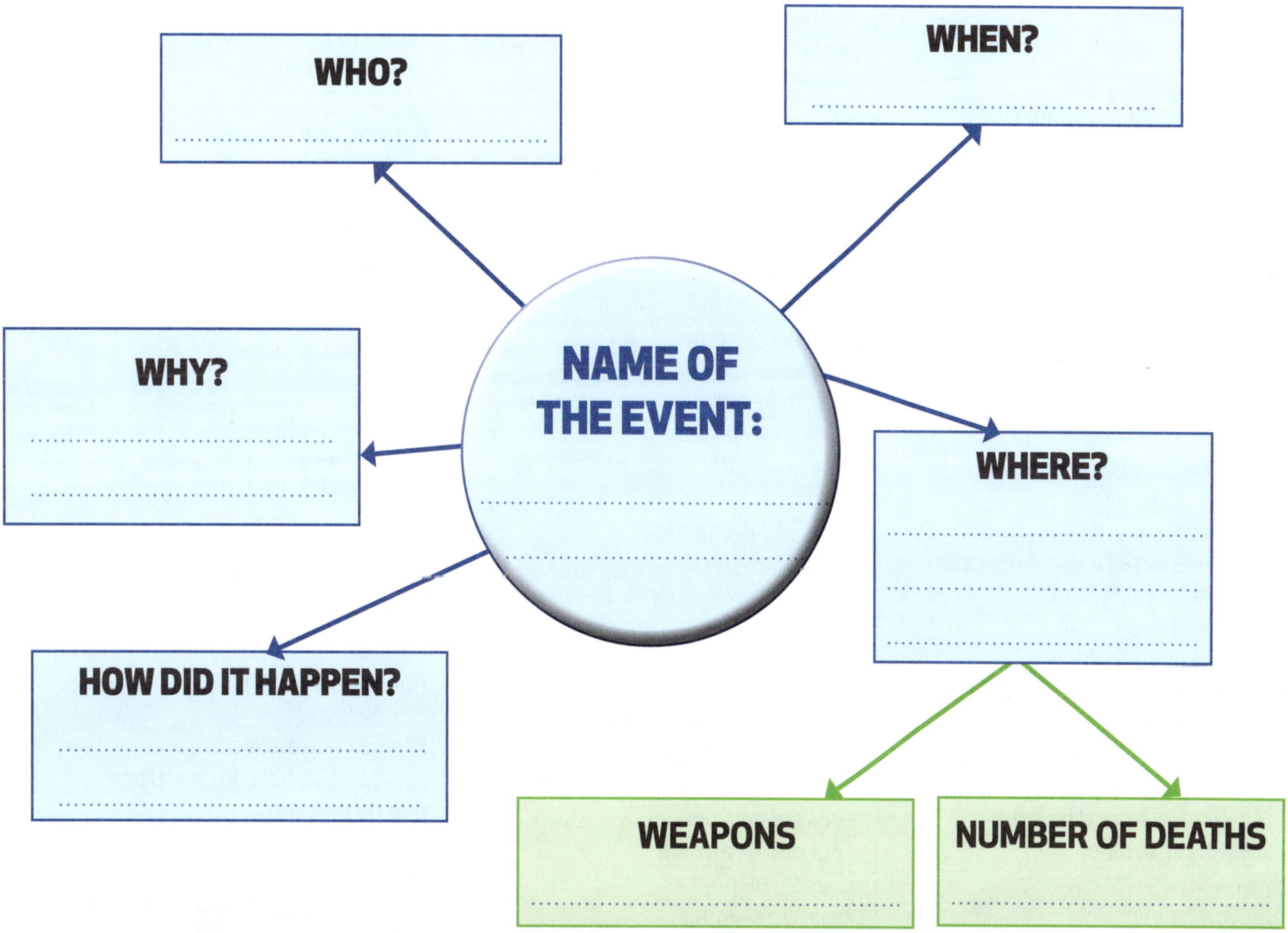

UNIT 10 Thrilling Stories

NOW ACT Page 116 exercise 5

Situation initiale (qui ? où ? quand ? quoi ?): ....

Élément perturbateur : ....

Péripéties : ....

Résolution : ....

Situation finale : ....

Lexique ANGLAIS-FRANÇAIS

Addressee un(e) destinataire
advice des conseils
already déjà
appease apaiser
appliance un appareil
app(lication) une appli(cation)
apprentice un(e) apprenti(e)
area la superficie
arrow une flèche
as soon as possible dès que possible
at (@) arobase
at the bottom en bas
at the top en haut
author un auteur

Background l'arrière-plan
backpack un sac à dos
ban interdire
bank une rive
battle une bataille
be* être
be* afraid avoir peur
be* cold avoir froid
be* divided into être divisé en
be* fond of aimer
be* hot avoir chaud
be* hungry avoir faim
be* on time être à l'heure
be* thirsty avoir soif
beans des haricots
become* devenir
beef du bœuf
begin* commencer
behave se comporter
behaviour attitude, comportement
belief une croyance
belong to appartenir à
big grand, important, gros
billionaire un milliardaire
booking une réservation
bookkeeper un(e) comptable
bootlegger un contrebandier
borough un district
bow un arc
bridge un pont
buckskin en peau de daim
build* construire, bâtir
building un bâtiment, un immeuble
burglary un cambriolage
bus tour une visite en bus

Can I help you? Que puis-je faire pour vous?
caption une légende (photo)
career une carrière (professionnelle)
caring *(adj.)* attentionné
cash de l'argent liquide
casual décontracté (vêtements)
challenging stimulant, éprouvant
character un personnage
charity une association, œuvre caritative
chat *(v)* tchatter
cheese du fromage
check vérifier
cheerful enjoué, joyeux
chicken du poulet
Chief Executive Officer (CEO) un PDG
clearly clairement
climate un climat
clothes les vêtements
CO_2 emissions des émissions de carbone
co-founder un(e) cofondateur(trice)
company une entreprise
consumption la consommation
contact details les coordonnées
cook *(v)* cuisiner
cool down refroidir
country un pays
creative créatif
cross traverser
currency la devise, la monnaie du pays
cycling tour une visite à vélo

Daily tous les jours
date back to remonter à
dead mort, décédé
defeat *(v)* battre, vaincre
depict représenter, dépeindre
design *(v)* concevoir
device un appareil, un dispositif
dig* up the hatchet déterrer la hache de guerre
display *(v)* afficher
DNA fingerprint une empreinte ADN
dot (.) un point (mail, site)
dozen une douzaine
draw* dessiner, tirer
draw* an identikit picture dresser un portrait-robot
draw* water puiser de l'eau
drink *(n)* une boisson
drink* *(v)* boire

Earphones des écouteurs
easy facile
email address une adresse électronique
emergency une urgence
enjoy aimer, apprécier
enthusiastic enthousiaste, passionné

Fabulous fabuleux, sensationnel
fact un fait
faith la foi
fast *(adj.)* rapide
favorite (US), favourite (UK) préféré
feather une plume
fight *(n)* une bagarre
fight* *(v)* se battre
find* trouver
firearm une arme à feu
firewood du bois de chauffage
fish du poisson
flag un drapeau
floor le sol, un étage
focus on se concentrer, se focaliser sur
fold plier
follower un(e) abonné(e)
food de la nourriture
footwear des chaussures
foreground le premier plan
forget* oublier
formal habillé (vêtements)
formerly anciennement
found fonder
founder un(e) fondateur(trice), un(e) créateur(trice)
funding un financement

Game un jeu, un sport
gentle gentil, doux
gift un cadeau
go* downstairs descendre (escaliers)

go* straight on aller tout droit
go* upstairs monter (escaliers)
goods des marchandises
gorgeous superbe, splendide
graduate *(n)* un(e) diplômé(e)
greet saluer
greeting un salut
grow* augmenter, faire grandir
guidelines des recommandations

Hate détester
have* avoir, posséder
have* (a drink) prendre (une boisson)
head la tête
headdress une coiffe
headquarters un siège social
health la santé
hear* entendre
heat chauffer
heiress une héritière
help *(n)* de l'aide
help *(v)* aider
hold* tenir
host *(n)* un(e) hôte(sse)
hot très chaud, épicé
how comment
hunter un chasseur
husband un mari

Improve améliorer
in case… au cas où…
in the middle au milieu
inhabitant un(e) habitant(e)
inherit hériter
injure blesser
innovative novateur
inside à l'intérieur
insurance une assurance
investigate enquêter
investor un investisseur
invoke invoquer
issue un problème, un enjeu
item un article (commerce)

Jewellery (UK), jewelry (US) des bijoux
jewels des bijoux
journey un voyage

Keep* garder, conserver
keep* watch faire le guet
key une clé
kidnap kidnapper
kind gentil
know* connaître, savoir

Laboratory un laboratoire
landmark un monument
launch *(v)* lancer
lead* mener, diriger
learn apprendre
left-hand (situé) à gauche
length la durée
let me know if… faites-moi savoir si…
lift *(n)* un ascenseur
like *(v)* aimer
litter les détritus
live vivre, habiter
lively animé, gai, vivant
located situé
lose* perdre
lost property office le bureau des objets trouvés
love *(v)* aimer
lunch break une pause déjeuner

Make* faire
meal un repas
medicine man un sorcier
megacity une métropole
middle ground le plan intermédiaire
mobster un truand
move déplacer
movement un mouvement
murder *(n)* un meurtre

Need *(v)* avoir besoin de
neighbour un(e) voisin(e)
never jamais
Nice to meet you Enchanté
nickname un surnom
noisy bruyant
not… yet pas encore
nurse un(e) infirmier(ère)

Occupation une profession, un métier
oil le pétrole
on the left à gauche
on the right à droite
opening times horaires d'ouverture
open-top sightseeing bus un bus touristique à impériale
order *(n)* une commande
order *(v)* commander
outfit une tenue
outside à l'extérieur

Pack faire ses bagages
parking spot une place de parking
partnership un partenariat
party *(v)* faire la fête
passport un passeport
password un mot de passe
past le passé
patrol *(v)* patrouiller
patron un donateur
pavement un trottoir
peace la paix
peace pipe un calumet de la paix
peaceful pacifique
perform réaliser, accomplir
phone number un numéro de téléphone
pillage piller
play *(v)* jouer
pleased ravi, content
plot une intrigue, un complot
plug *(n)* une prise électrique
plug adapter un adaptateur
polluting polluant
popular populaire
postcard une carte postale
prayer une prière
press presser, serrer
prevent empêcher
price un prix (argent)
product un produit
prop un accessoire (théâtre)
properly correctement
provide fournir
punctual ponctuel
purchase *(v)* acheter
purpose un but

Qualified qualifié

Ransom une rançon
raven un corbeau
recycle recycler
recycling waste collector une colonne de recyclage
reduce réduire
refine raffiner
release *(v)* sortir (film, musique)
rely on compter sur

rent *(v)* louer
repeal une abrogation, une révocation
reservation une réserve (zone), réservation (hôtel)
rice du riz
ride* a bike faire du vélo
rifle un fusil
right *(adj.)* correct, bon, juste
right-hand (situé) à droite
river tour une visite en bateau
roaring rugissant
roll *(v)* rouler, enrouler
rule *(n)* une règle, loi
rule *(v)* gouverner
run* courir, diriger (un pays)

Safe sûr, sécurisé
safety issue un problème de sécurité
salesperson un(e) vendeur(euse)
sales representative un représentant commercial
schedule des horaires, un emploi du temps
seat un siège
sender un expéditeur
sensor un capteur
settler un colon (hist.)
share partager
shop un magasin, une boutique
shopper un client
shout *(v)* crier
shrimp une crevette
sign up s'inscrire, s'abonner
silk la soie
single seul(e), célibataire
situated situé
skilled *(adj.)* expérimenté
skills des compétences
slavery l'esclavage
slide show un diaporama
smart (US) intelligent **(UK)** élégant
sneakers des baskets
social media les réseaux sociaux
soft *(adj.)* doux
software un / des logiciels
soldier un soldat
space l'espace
speakeasy un bar clandestin
spirit un esprit
sportswear des vêtements de sport
stairs un escalier, des marches
stamp un timbre
start commencer
step un pas
store un magasin
story une histoire
street une rue
stressed tendu
student un(e) étudiant(e)
study étudier
stunning éblouissant, sensationnel
successful prospère, à succès
suitcase une valise
symbolically symboliquement

Take* prendre
take* away emporter
take* control of prendre le contrôle de
take* fingerprints relever des empreintes
tall grand
target une cible
task une tâche
tax evasion la fraude fiscale
tea du thé
tens of des dizaines de
thank remercier
thousands of des milliers de
tired fatigué
tomorrow demain
trade le commerce
traffic congestion un embouteillage
trainee un(e) stagiaire
travel *(v)* voyager
treaty un traité
tribe une tribu
turn left tourner à gauche
turn off éteindre
turn right tourner à droite
tutor un(e) tuteur(trice)
twice deux fois
twist un renversement de situation

Upgrade mettre à jour, à niveau
useful utile
user un(e) utilisateur(trice)
user ID un identifiant

Vocational school un lycée professionnel

Wait for attendre
waiter un serveur
waitress une serveuse
walking tour une visite à pied
walk past passer devant
warpath le sentier de la guerre
warrior un guerrier
wastes les ordures
way un chemin, une direction, façon (de faire)
weapon une arme
wear* porter (des vêtements)
website un site internet
welcome *(v)* accueillir
welcome! *(interj.)* bienvenue !
well-known bien connu
what quoi, que, quel
wheel une roue
where où
which quel, lequel, lesquels
who qui
whose dont, à qui
why pourquoi
wife une épouse
work placement un stage
worldwide dans le monde entier
write* écrire

Yesterday hier
yet cependant

Lexique

FRANÇAIS-ANGLAIS

A **Abonné(e)** a follower
s'abonner sign up
accessoire *(théâtre)* a prop
accomplir perform
accueillir welcome
acheter purchase
adaptateur *(élect.)* a plug adapter
adresse électronique an email address
afficher display
aide help
aider help
aimer like, be* fond of
aimer, adorer love
aller tout droit go* straight on
améliorer improve
anciennement formerly
animé lively
apaiser appease
appareil an appliance, a device
appli(cation) an app(lication)
appartenir à belong to
apprécier enjoy
apprendre learn
apprenti(e) an apprentice
arc a bow
argent liquide cash
arme a weapon
arme à feu a firearm
arobase at (@)
arrière-plan the background
article *(commerce)* an item
ascenseur a lift
association (caritative) a charity
assurance an insurance
attendre wait for
attentionné caring
attitude a behaviour
au cas où… in case…
augmenter grow*
auteur an author
avoir, posséder have*
avoir besoin de need
avoir chaud be* hot
avoir faim be* hungry
avoir froid be* cold
avoir peur be* afraid
avoir soif be* thirsty

B **Baccalauréat professionnel** BTEC National Diploma (UK)
bagarre a fight
bar clandestin a speakeasy
baskets sneakers
bataille a battle
bâtiment a building
bâtir build*
battre defeat
(se) battre (contre) fight* (against)
bien connu well-known
Bienvenue! Welcome!
bijoux jewellery (UK), jewelry (US)
blesser injure
bœuf beef
boire drink*
bois de chauffage firewood
boisson a drink
boutique a shop (UK), a store (US)
bruyant noisy
bureau des objets trouvés lost property office
bus touristique à impériale an open-top sightseeing bus
but a purpose

C **Cadeau** a gift
calumet de la paix a peace pipe
cambriolage a burglary
capteur a sensor
carrière a career
carte postale a postcard
célibataire *(adj.)* single
cependant yet
chasseur a hunter
chaud hot
chauffer heat
chaussures shoes, footwear
chemin a way
cible a target
clairement clearly
clé a key
client(e) a shopper, a customer
climat a climate
cofondateur(trice) a co-founder
coiffe a headdress
colon *(hist.)* a settler
colonnes à recycler recycling waste collectors
combattre fight* (against)
commande an order
commander order
commencer begin*, start
comment how
compétences skills
complot a plot
comportement a behavior (US), behaviour (UK)
(se) comporter behave
comptable a bookkeeper
compter sur rely on
(se) concentrer sur focus on
concevoir design
connaître know*
conseils advice
conserver keep*
construire build*
consommation consumption
content pleased, happy
contrebandier a bootlegger
coordonnées contact details
corbeau a raven
correct right
correctement properly
créateur a founder
créatif creative
crevette a shrimp
crier shout
croyance a belief
cuisiner cook

D **Dans le monde entier** worldwide
décédé dead
décontracté (vêtements) casual
déjà already
demain tomorrow
dépeindre depict
déplacer move
dès que possible as soon as possible
descendre (escaliers) go* downstairs
dessiner draw*
destinataire an addressee
déterrer la hache de guerre dig* up the hatchet
détritus (des) litter
détester hate
deux fois twice
devenir become*
devise (monnaie du pays) currency
diaporama a slide show
diplomé *(n)* a graduate
direction the way
diriger (un pays) run*

dispositif a device
district a borough
dizaines de tens of
donateur a patron
dont ***(pron.)*** whose
douzaine a dozen
doux soft
drapeau a flag
dresser un portrait-robot draw* an identikit picture
(à) droite on the right, right-hand
durée length

Eblouissant stunning
écrire write*
écouteurs earphones
effondrement collapse
élégant smart
embouteillage a traffic congestion
embuscade (tendre une) ambush
émissions de carbone CO_2 emissions
empêcher prevent
emploi du temps a schedule
emporter take* away
empreinte ADN a DNA fingerprint
en bas at the bottom
en haut at the top
en peau de daim buckskin
Enchanté Nice to meet you
enjoué, joyeux cheerful
enquêter investigate
enrouler roll
entendre hear*
enthousiaste enthusiastic
entreprise a company
épicé hot
épouse a wife
éprouvant challenging
escalier stairs
esclavage slavery
espace a space
esprit a spirit
étage a floor
éteindre turn off
(s')étrangler choke
être be*
être à l'heure be* on time
être divisé en be* divided into
(s')étouffer choke
étudiant(e) a student
étudier study
expéditeur a sender
expérimenté skilled

(à l')extérieur outside

Fabuleux fabulous
fabriquer make*
facile easy
façon (de faire) a way
faire make*, do
faire de la contrebande smuggle
faire de l'exercice take* exercise
faire du vélo ride* a bike
faire grandir grow*
faire la fête party
faire le guet keep* watch
faire ses bagages pack
fait ***(n)*** a fact
faites moi savoir si… let me know if...
fatigué tired
financement a funding
flèche an arrow
(se) focaliser sur focus on
fondateur a founder
fonder found
fournir provide
fraude fiscale tax evasion
fromage cheese
fusil a rifle

Garder keep*
(à) gauche on the left, left-hand
gentil gentle, kind
gouverner rule
grand big
grand (de grande taille) tall
gros big
guerrier a warrior

Habitant(e) an inhabitant
habiter live
haricots beans
hériter inherit
héritièr(e) an heir(ess)
hier yesterday
histoire a story
horaires (de travail) a schedule
horaires d'ouverture opening hours
hôte(sse) a host

Identifiant a user id
immeuble a building
important important, big
infirmier(ère) a nurse
s'inscrire sign up

intelligent smart (US), intelligent, clever (UK)
interdire ban
(à l')intérieur inside
intrigue a plot
investisseur an investor
invoquer invoke

Jamais never
jeu (sport) a game
jouer play
juste right, fair

Kidnapper kidnap

Laboratoire a laboratory
lancer (un produit) launch
légende (photo) a caption
lequel(le), lesquel(le)s which
logiciel(s) software
loi a rule, a law
louer rent
lycée professionnel a vocational school

Magasin a shop (UK), a store (US)
marchandises goods
marches stairs
mari a husband
métier an occupation, a job
métropole a megacity
meurtre a murder
milliardaire a billionaire
milliers de thousands of
(au) milieu (in the) middle
mise à jour an upgrade
monter (escaliers) go* upstairs
monument a landmark
mouvement a movement
mort ***(adj.)*** dead
mot de passe a password

Nourriture food
novateur ***(adj.)*** innovant
numéro de téléphone a phone number

Obligatoire compulsory
œuvre caritative a charity
ordures wastes
où where
oublier forget*

Pacifique peaceful
paix peace
pas *(n)* a step
passeport a passport
passer devant walk past
passé *(n)* the past
pause déjeuner a lunch break
partager share
partenariat a partnership
patrouiller patrol
pays a country
PDG a Chief Executive Officer (CEO)
perdre lose*
personnage a character
pétrole oil
piller pillage
place de parking a parking spot
plan intermédiaire the middle ground
plier fold
plume a feather
point (mail, site) a dot (.)
poisson fish
polluant polluting
pont a bridge
ponctuel punctual
populaire popular
porter (des vêtements) wear*
poulet chicken
pourquoi why
préféré favorite (US), favourite (UK)
premier plan the foreground
prendre take*
prendre le contrôle de take* control of
prendre (une boisson) have* (a drink)
presser press
prière a prayer
prise électrique a plug
prix (argent) a price
problème de sécurité a safety issue
produit a product
profession an occupation, a job
prospère successful
puiser de l'eau draw* water

Qualifié *(adj.)* qualified
quand when
que what
Que puis-je faire pour vous ? Can I help you?
quel(le), quel(le)s which, what
qui who
(à) qui whose
quoi what

Raffiner refine
ravi pleased
rançon a ransom
rapide *(adj.)* fast
réaliser perform
recommandations guidelines
recycler recycle
réduire reduce
refroidir cool down
règle a rule
relever des empreintes take* fingerprints
remercier thank
remonter à date back to
renversement de situation a twist
repas a meal
représentant (commercial) a sales representative
représenter depict
réseaux sociaux social media
réservation a booking, a reservation
réserve (zone) a reservation
rive a bank
riz rice
roue a wheel
rouler roll
rue a street
rugissant roaring

Sac à dos a backpack
salut a greeting
santé health
savoir know*
sécurisé safe
sensationnel fabulous, stunning
sentier de la guerre the warpath
serrer press
serveur(se) waiter(tress)
seul single
siège a seat
siège social headquarters
site internet a website
situé situated, located
soie silk
soldat a soldier
sorcier a medicine man
sortir (film, musique) release
stage a work placement
stagiaire a trainee
stimulant challenging
(à) succès successful
superbe gorgeous
superficie the area
sûr safe
surnom a nickname
symboliquement symbolically
système a device

Tâche a task
tchatter chat
tendu stressed
tenir hold*
tenue *(n)* an outfit
thé tea
timbre a stamp
tirer draw*
tourner à droite turn right
tourner à gauche turn left
tous les jours daily
traité *(n)* a treaty
traverser cross
tribu a tribe
trottoir a pavement
trouver find*
truand a mobster
tuteur(trice) a tutor

Urgence an emergency
utile useful
utilisateur(trice) a user

Valise a suitcase
vaincre defeat
vendeur/vendeuse a salesperson
vérifier check
vêtements clothes
vêtements de sport sportswear
visite à pied a walking tour
visite à vélo a cycling tour
visite en bateau a river tour
visite en bus a bus tour
vivre live
voisin(e) a neighbour
voyage a journey
voyager travel

Crédits photographiques

PAGES
3 haut ph © whitemay/iStockphoto (reprise p 31 haut gauche)
3 bas ph © contrastwerkstatt/stock.adobe.com (reprise p 43 bas_1)
4 haut ph © Instants/iStockphoto (reprise p 55 bas gauche)
4 bas ph © fotoVoyager/iStockphoto (reprise p 65 bas droite_1)
5 haut ph © zimmytws/iStockphoto (reprise p 79 milieu)
5 bas ph © Alamy/Photo12 (reprise p 9[illegible]d)
6 haut Underwood Archives/Collectio[n] Christophel (reprise p 103 milieu gauche)
6 bas ph © AI/Fotolia (reprise p 115 h[a]ut droite)
7 haut droite ph © Kristen Sarah - [ho]pscotchtheglobe.com - youtube.com/hopscotchthe[gl]obe
7 milieu gauche ph © Kristen Sa[rah] - hopscotchtheglobe.com - yout[ube].com/hopscotchtheglobe
7 bas droite ph © Thomas Rei[...]er/stock.adobe.com
8 ph © Matton
9 haut gauche ph © silverkb[l]ack/Fotolia
9 haut droite ph © Kit Via[tk]ins/Fotolia
9 milieu_1, 2, 3 et 4 ph © [Kit] Viatkins/Fotolia
11 ph © Bepsimage/iStoc[k]photo
12 page entière ph © M[at]ton
13 gauche ph © Djessi[...]3/Fotolia
13 droite ph © Matto[n]
14 ph © semevent/s[to]ck.adobe.com
15 ph © Matton
16 haut gauche ph © Michael Flippo/stock.adobe.com
16 haut milieu ph © Kurhan/Fotolia
16 haut droite ph © antgor/stock.adobe.com
16 bas gauche ph © JackF/Fotolia
16 bas milieu ph © lenets_tan/Fotolia
16 bas droite ph © Юлия Завалишина/Fotolia
17 portrait ph © ewg3D/iStockphoto
17 miniatures ph © Matton
19_1 ph © Matton
19_2 ph © nmcandre/Fotolia
19_3 ph © Matton
20 haut gauche 1 et 2 ph © Matton
20 haut gauche_3 ph © Sozh/Fotolia
20 bas 1 ph © Grafikwerkstatt Köln/Fotolia
20 bas 2 ph © Matton
20 bas 3 ph © conceptcafe/Fotolia
20 bas 4 ph © dneprstock/Fotolia
20 bas 5 ph © massimo_g/Fotolia
22 a et c ph © Jackin/Fotolia
22 b ph © andriano_cz/Fotolia
22 autres ph © Matton
23_a ph © nelelena/stock.adobe.com
23_c ph © alexlmx
25 haut ph © Visual Generation/Shutterstock
25 milieu ph © Chlorophylle/Fotolia
25 bas ph © patcharee11/Fotolia
26 ph © Syda Productions/stock.adobe.com
27 haut gauche_1 ph © Sirena Designs/stock.adobe.com
27 haut droite_1 ph © herreid/iStockphoto
27 haut gauche_2 ph © william87/stock.adobe.com
27 haut droite_1 ph © wundervisuals/iStockphoto
27 milieu ph © michaeljung
27 bas ph © Matton
28 haut ph © Alamy/Photo12
28 bas ph © Image Source/iStockphoto
31 milieu ph © Matton
31 haut gauche ph © whitemay/iStockphoto (reprise p 3 haut)
31 haut droite ph © tirc83/iStockphoto
31 bas gauche ph © paulafrench/iStockphoto
31 bas droite ph © Maridav/stock.adobe.com
32 haut ph © Matton
32 a ph © Granger NYC/Aurimages
32 b ph © Rixipix/iStockphoto
32 c ph © Heritage Images/Leemage
32 d ph © Alamy/Photo12
32 e ph © nata_zhekova/Fotolia
32 bas ph © Matton
33 gauche ph © kylieellway/iStockphoto
33 milieu ph © Sam Spiro/Fotolia
33 droite ph © PA Photos/Abaca
34 ph © Matton
36 ph © Matton
37 ph © f11photo/iStockphoto
38 ph © olive1976/stock.adobe.com
39 haut ph © Matton
39 bas ph © vichie81/stock.adobe.com
40 haut ph © Alamy/Photo12
40 bas ph © Alamy/Photo12
41 haut ph © Monkey Business/stock.adobe.com
41 bas ph © Matton
42_1 ph © Mumpitz/stock.adobe.com
42_2 ph © bunwit/stock.adobe.com
42_3 ph © Oliver Preißner/stock.adobe.com
42_4 ph © belyjmishka/stock.adobe.com
42_5 ph © Jenner/stock.adobe.com
42_6 ph © Matton
42 bas ph © Matton
43_a, b, c et d ph © Matton
43 bas_1 ph © contrastwerkstatt/stock.adobe.com (reprise p 3 bas)
43 bas_2 ph © Matton
44 ph © Matton
46_a ph © Maos/stock.adobe.com
46_b, c, d, e et f ph © Matton
47 ph © Matton
49 milieu ph © Baillou/stock.adobe.com
49 bas ph © Wisiel/stock.adobe.com
50 ph © irinastrel123/stock.adobe.com
51 haut ph © The LIFE Picture Collection/Getty Images
51 bas ph © Cui hao/Imaginechina/AFP
52 haut ph © D Dipasupil/Getty Images/AFP
52 bas ph © collection Christophel © Forward pass / Appian way, The aviator, 2005, réalisation Martin Scorsese
55 haut gauche ph © Matton (reprise p 60_3)
55 haut droit ph © Uma Kadam/The Times of India/AFP
55 bas gauche ph © Instants/iStockphoto (reprise p 4 haut)
56 haut ph © hansslegers/iStockphoto
56 bas droite ph © NataliaDeriabina/iStockphoto
56 bas milieu ph © Sujay_Govindaraj/iStockphoto
56 bas droite ph © DrRave/iStockphoto
57 haut gauche ph © manx_in_the_world/iStockphoto
57 haut milieu ph © Granger NYC/Rue des Archives
57 haut droit ph © SuperStock/Leemage
57 milieu gauche ph © zlatovlaska2008/stock.adobe.com
57 milieu droit ph © ISRO - Indian Space Research Organization
58 ph © collection Christophel © Aka Mediaworks, *Baahubali 2 The conclusion*, 2017, réalisation SS Rajamouli Prabhas
60_1, 2, 4 et 7 ph © Matton
60_3 ph © Matton (reprise p 55 haut gauche)
60_5 ph © 3d_generator/stock.adobe.com
60_6 ph © Logorilla/iStockphoto
61 gauche ph © pavalena/iStockphoto
61 milieu gauche ph © hadynyah/iStockphoto
61 milieu droit ph © Matton
61 droite ph © Matton
63 haut gauche ph © Jason Magerkorth/iStockphoto
63 haut milieu ph © naruedom/iStockphoto
63 haut droit ph © Matton
64 ph © Matton
65 haut droite_1 ph © Sterling750/iStockphoto
65 haut droite_2 ph © Matton (reprise p 99 haut droite_2)
65 haut droite_1 ph © Easyturn/iStockphoto
65 haut droite_2 ph © Matton
65 bas droite_1 ph © fotoVoyager/iStockphoto (reprise p 4 bas)
65 bas droite_2 ph © Matton
66 haut gauche ph © thanasus/iStockphoto
66 haut milieu © Citymapper
66 haut droit ph © MicroOne/Fotolia
66 bas ph © ferrantraite/iStockphoto
67 haut milieu ph © Cerbi/iStockphoto
67 milieu gauche ph © Maksim Pasko/Fotolia
67 milieu droit ph © panitialapon/Fotolia
68 ph © Michael Rosskothen/Fotolia
69 ph © VRD/Fotolia
70 gauche ph © Scanrail/stock.adobe.com
70 milieu gauche ph © Destina/stock.adobe.com
70 milieu droite ph © Standard/REX/Shutterstock/Sipa
70 droite ph © robu_s/stock.adobe.com
73_1 ph © dikobrazik/Fotolia
73_2 ph © Alamy/Photo12
73_3 © www.wien.info
73_4 ph © ymgerman/Fotolia
73_5 ph © Jamrooferpix/Fotolia
73_6 ph © Tramino/iStockphoto
73_7 © The MAKCi Awards - The World Capital Institute
73_8 ph © Matton
73 bas_1 ph © Mnaniti/Fotolia
73 bas_2 ph © svetikd/iStockphoto
73 bas_3 ph © Matton
73 bas_4 ph © Matton
74 ph © saiko3p/iStockphoto
75 haut gauche ph © Matton
75 haut droite ph © Matton
75 milieu gauche ph © BL
75 milieu droite ph © BL
75 bas gauche ph © Mafuta/iStockphoto
75 bas droite ph © BL
76 haut ph © Louise Gubb/The Image Works/Roger-Viollet
76 milieu ph © RapidEye/iStockphoto
76 bas ph © pawopa3336/stock.adobe.com
78 ph © Matton
79 milieu ph © zimmytws/iStockphoto (reprise p 5 haut)
79 haut gauche ph © bennymarty/iStockphoto
79 haut droite ph © JasonDoiy/iStockphoto
79 bas gauche ph © JasonDoiy/iStockphoto
79 bas droite ph © JasonDoiy/iStockphoto
80 haut © Gametime United, Inc.
80 bas ph © Cédric Jacquot/PHOTOPQR/L'EST REPUBLICAIN/MAXPP
81 ph © Solent News/SIPA
82 ph © Amy Lombard/The New York Times-REDUX-REA
84 ph © Matton
85 haut gauche ph © kange_one/Fotolia
85 haut droite ph © Ilya_Starikov/iStockphoto
85 bas gauche ph © David Paul Morris/Getty Images
85 bas droite ph © Renault for Car Body Design
87 haut gauche ph © Lucy Nicholson/Reuters
87 haut droite ph © J. Emilio Flores/The New York Times-REDUX-REA
87 milieu gauche ph © Matton
87 bas gauche ph © Bloomberg/Getty Images
87 bas droite ph © Wachiwit/iStockphoto
88 ph © mbbirdy/iStockphoto
89_1 ph © Granger NYC / Bridgeman Images
89_2 ph © coll. LR/adoc photos
89_3 ph © Bridgeman Images, photographie de David Frances Barry (1854-1934) coll. privée
89_4 ph © Tarrant County College NE, Heritage Room
90 haut gauche ph © Buyenlarge/Getty Images
90 haut droite ph © Nationalclothing.org
90 bas ph © Granger/Bridgeman Images
91_a ph © Peter Newark American Pictures/Bridgeman Images, lithographie de George Catlin (1796-1872) coll. privée (a)
91_b ph © akg-images
91_c ph © jozefklopacka/stock.adobe.com
91_d ph © Bridgeman Images; Rob Wood, Plains Indian, guardian spirit, 2004
91 bas ph © Education Images/UIG/agefotostock.com
92 ph © Universal Images Group Editorial/Getty Images
94_1 ph © Charles Butzin/Fotolia
94_2 ph © Kotliar Ivan/Fotolia
94_3 ph © kiberstalker/Fotolia
94_4 ph © Andrey Burmakin/Fotolia
94_5 ph © BillionPhotos.com/Fotolia
94_6 ph © HN Works/Fotolia
94_7 ph © Matton
94_8 ph © Matton
95_a ph © Interfoto/La Collection
95_b ph © Plimoth Plantation
95_c ph © Alamy/Photo12
95_d ph © Alamy/Photo12 (reprise page 5 bas)
97 haut ph © collection particulière
97 bas ph © Granger NYC / Bridgeman Images
98 haut milieu ph © Regina Fraser et Pat Johnson
99 haut gauche ph © Matton
99 haut droite 1 ph © PeterHermesFurian/iStockphoto
99 haut droite_2 ph © Matton (reprise p 65 haut droite_2)
99 bas gauche ph © Charles McQuillan/Getty Images
99 bas droite ph © Paul J Martin/Shutterstock
100 ph © Paul Faith/PA Archive/PA Images/Abaca
103 haut gauche ph © collection Christophel © Corman Co/Los Altos Productions, The St Valentine's day massacre, 1967, réalisation Roger Corman
103 haut droite_1 ph © DA69/iStockphoto
103 milieu gauche ph © Underwood Archives/collection Christophel (reprise page 6 haut)
103 milieu droite ph © NY Daily News Archive/Getty Images
103 haut droite_2 ph © sergiibobliakh/stock.adobe.com
104 haut_1 ph © Fotosearch/Getty Images
104 haut_2 ph © Tony Baggett/stock.adobe.com
104 haut_3 ph © Lalnspiratriz/stock.adobe.com
104 haut_4 ph © Mary Evans/Rue des Archives
104 bas gauche ph © collection particulière, F. Scott Fitzgerald *Great Gatsby* Cover of the first edition in 1925. Charles Scribner's Sons, illustration de couverture Francis Cugat
105 haut gauche ph © Bettmann Archive/Getty Images
105 haut milieu ph © Bettmann Archive/Getty Images
105 haut droite ph © Bridgeman Images
105 bas ph © Lalnspiratriz/stock.adobe.com
106 ph © Rue des Archives/RDA
107 ph © Keystone France/Gamma-Rapho
108 ph © aleutie/stock.adobe.com
109 ph © vgorbash/stock.adobe.com
110 ph © medejaja/stock.adobe.com
111 haut ph © collection Christophel © Warner Bros/ Village Roadshow Pictures, *The Great Gatsby*, 2013, réalisation Baz Luhrmann
111 bas ph © collection Christophel/RnB © Warner Bros, *Angels with dirty faces*, 1938, réalisation Michael Curtiz
112 haut ph © collection Christophel © Mediapro/ Versatil Cinema, *Midnight in Paris*, 2011, réalisation Woody Allen
112 bas ph © collection Christophel/RnB © Ladd Company, *Once Upon a Time in America*, 1984, réalisation Sergio Leone
113 haut gauche ph © collection Christophel © Lin Pictures Silver Pictures/Village Roadshow Pictures/ Wigram Productions, *Sherlock Holmes*, 2009, réalisation Guy Ritchie
113 haut droite ph © collection Christophel © ABC Studios/ShondaLand/NoWalk Entertainment, *How to Get Away with Murder*, série créée par Peter Nowalk
114 haut © Penguin Random House
114 bas a, b et c ph © Collection Christophe/RnB -® Alfred J Hitchcock Productions, *The Birds*, 1963 réalisation Alfred HitchcockRod Taylor.
115 haut gauche ph © Sasenki/Fotolia
115 haut milieu ph © Matton
115 haut droite ph © AI/Fotolia (reprise p 6 bas)
115 milieu gauche ph © PanovA/Fotolia
115 milieu droite ph © grandeduc/Fotolia
116 ph © Constantin Fülle/iStockphoto
118 ph © i-picture/stock.adobe.com
121 haut ph © Collection Christophel © Mednick Productions, *Devil's Gate*, 2017, réalisation Clay Staub
121 bas ph © Collection Christophel ©Edici/Penciller Pictures *The Chamber*, 2016, réalisation Ben Parker Collection Christophel © Edici/Penciller Pictures
122 haut gauche © Penguin Random House
122 haut milieu ph © Matton
122 bas ph © tuiphotoengineer/Fotolia
123_1 ph © Historic England/Bridgeman Images Rembrandt van Rijn (1606-69), *Self Portrait*, c.1665, The Iveagh Bequest, Kenwood House
123_2 ph © Bridgeman Images, Vincent van Gogh (1853-90), *Self Portrait with Bandaged Ear*, 1889, Samuel Courtauld Trust, The Courtauld Gallery
123_3 ph © Lefevre Fine Art Ltd., London/Bridgeman Images, Claude Monet (1840-1926) *Self Portrait with a Beret*, 1886, coll. privée
123_4 © Succession Picasso 2018 ph © Christie's Images/Bridgeman Images, Pablo Picasso (1881-1973) *Buste d'homme écrivant (Autoportrait)*, 1971, coll. privée
123_5 © Adagp, Paris 2018, ph © Christie's Images/ Bridgeman Images, René Magritte (1898-1967) *The Son of Man*, 1964, coll. privée
124 haut © The Estate of Francis Bacon - All rights reserved/Adagp, Paris and DACS, London, 2018, ph © Centre Pompidou, MNAM-CCI, Dist. RMN-Grand Palais/Philippe Migeat, Francis Bacon Francis (1909-1992) *Autoportrait*, 1971
124 bas © Succession Picasso 2018 ph © Christie's Images/Bridgeman Images, Pablo Picasso (1881-1973) *Head of a Man (Self-portrait)* 1964, coll. privée
126 ph © Kablonk Micro/Fotolia
127 bas gauche ph © avoni/stock.adobe.com
127 bas droite ph © giorgiomtb/stock.adobe.com
129 et 130 ph © Alamy/Photo12
131-132 haut gauche ph © Matton
131-132 haut droite ph © Matton
131-132 bas droite_1 ph © LUKASZ-NOWAK1/iStockphoto
131-132 bas droite_2 ph © Saya King
133 ph © Collection Christophel © Pathe, *Devdas*, 2002, réalisation Sanjay Leela Bhansali
134 haut ph © Matton
134 milieu gauche ph © Obak/stock.adobe.com
134 milieu droite ph © Luciano Mortula-LGM/stock.adobe.com
135 haut gauche ph © Studio-Annika/iStockphoto
135 haut droite ph © Grafissimo/iStockphoto
135 bas gauche ph © nico_blue/iStockphoto
135 bas droite ph © jane/iStockphoto
136 ph © jörn buchheim/stock.adobe.com

Conception graphique Massimo Miola
Mise en pages Catherine Roussel
Iconographie Sophie Suberbère
Relecture Victoria Britten
Photogravure STDI
Illustrations Alfonso Recio
Cartographie Vincent Landrin

Paris – Mars 2018 – 01 – NB-CB / EG

Achevé d'imprimer en France par Loire Offset Titoulet à Saint-Etienne - France
Dépôt légal n° 14844-8/01 - février 2018